# GLASGOW
# TROLLEYBUSES

## Colin Barker

*Series editor Robert J Harley*

**MP** **Middleton Press**

*Front cover: At the Riddrie terminal stand in Maxwelton Road, Sunbeam TG10 waits before leaving for Rutherglen on Service 101. The handsome bodywork was by Weymann, and this batch of trolleybuses, delivered in 1953, were the first Glasgow double deckers on two axles. The "via" blind aperture has been panelled over as an economy measure; many other vehicles had this glass area below the destination painted over. (G Lumb/Travel Lens Photographic)*

*Rear cover: On a return trip to Hampden Garage via Mount Florida, TBS13 has just left Paisley Road Toll, and is seen leaving Scotland Street to begin the long climb up Shields Road on Service 108. The ten vehicles from this batch, delivered in 1958, were 34.5ft (10.5m) long, exceeding the then legal limit, and were fitted with bodies by Burlingham, incorporating a single front entrance/ exit. TBS13 is the sole survivor, and was exhibited at Glasgow's original Museum of Transport, and then later in the Kelvin Hall replacement. Currently it is in store, rather than appearing in the new Riverside Transport Museum. The buildings to the rear have been replaced by the M8 Motorway. (Travel Lens Photographic)*

*Published November 2016*

*ISBN 978 1 908174 96 3*

*© Middleton Press, 2016*

*Design Cassandra Morgan*

*Published by*
    *Middleton Press*
    *Easebourne Lane*
    *Midhurst*
    *West Sussex*
    *GU29 9AZ*
*Tel: 01730 813169*
*Email: info@middletonpress.co.uk*
*www.middletonpress.co.uk*

*Printed and bound by CPI Group (UK) Ltd, Croydon, CR0 4YY*

# CONTENTS

# INTRODUCTION AND ACKNOWLEDGMENTS

The Glasgow trolleybus system was somewhat of an enigma. It was the only post Second World War system to be opened, the last in the UK, and took nine years to reach its maximum size of 43.5 route miles (70 km). It lasted a short 18 years in all, and was hastily abandoned, with perfectly good eight year old vehicles being sold for scrap!

The bodywork of the first 64 vehicles was the same as that fitted to trolleybuses produced for London Transport, and the Corporation was famous for its experiments with high capacity single deckers, none of which were entirely successful. Electricity was supplied from the Corporation's own Pinkston Power Station until 1958, whereas the rest of the electricity supply industry had been nationalised in the late 1940s.

Although the trolleybuses replaced a small number of tram services, there was still a large number of the latter operating, which were eventually replaced by motorbuses. Running trams, which had bow style current collection, caused some operational difficulties for trolleybuses, especially in narrow streets, and where they crossed trolleybus overhead wiring. Glasgow was the last place in the UK where trams and trolleybuses could be seen operating together.

All these factors have made this assignment particularly interesting and, having never seen the system in operation, I am indebted to Brian Deans, an acknowledged authority on Glasgow trolleybuses, for answering my interminable questions and queries; his earlier publications on the subject proved to be a valuable source of reference material. Without his input this publication would not have been possible.

This album is not intended to be a detailed history of the system, but more a pictorial journey along the routes that the trolleybuses served. Thanks go to photographers, copyright holders and collection owners who have generously allowed their material to be used, and due accreditation has been given where known. I have been unable to trace the origin of some photographs, and trust the photographers will accept their work has been used with good intent to add to the pictorial content.

In addition to answering all my questions, Brian Deans agreed to read through the first draft manuscript, together with Stewart Brown and Stuart Little; their input has been invaluable. The line drawings are by Terry Russell, maps prepared by Roger Smith, timetables/fare charts from the Omnibus Society Library, and tickets supplied by Eric Old; my thanks go to them for their assistance. Yet again, I must thank my wife Maureen for the use of her computer skills in converting my handiwork into the publisher's format, and her overall support whilst working on this assignment.

# HISTORICAL AND GEOGRAPHICAL SETTING

Glasgow's history goes back to earliest times, with evidence from the Stone Age, and a Roman presence in the area. A Christian church was established in the 6th century on the site of the current Cathedral, and legend suggests that St Mungo performed four miracles in the city.

By the end of the 12th century the population was estimated to have reached 1500; in 1451 the University was established, and soon the city had become an important ecclesiastical and academic centre.

The 16th and 17th century saw Glasgow's importance increase, with its wealth continuing to grow, in spite of episodes of the plague, and city fires. Shipping access to the Irish Sea and Atlantic Ocean, and onward to the Americas, became important; the first tobacco was imported in 1674. In the 18th century Glasgow became famous for its linen, and cotton spinning developed as a major industry.

By the 19th century, the influence of the Industrial Revolution was being felt, with the growth of a whole range of manufacturing processes, many using locally produced coal to power steam driven machinery. The city also embraced heavy engineering including locomotive production and shipbuilding, the latter producing one fifth of the world's ships from the late 1800s up to the outbreak of the First World War. This was the period when many of the city's public buildings and open spaces were created, and by 1851 the population had reached about 329,000.

The 20th century saw major economic decline after the First World War, with the city being classed as a depressed area in the 1930s. There was a decline in locomotive production and shipbuilding; the latter recovered for a short period after the Second World War, but the sector continued to decline as a result of more competitive pricing from emerging nations.

Culturally, there were major events in the 1980/1990s including the opening of the Burrell Centre, Scottish Exhibition and Conference Centre, Glasgow Garden Festival, Royal Concert Hall and culminating in the city becoming European City of Culture in 1990. The city's re-generation has continued into the 21st century.

Glasgow sits astride the River Clyde in the southern Scottish Lowlands, with access to the Highlands to the north, and Edinburgh to the east. The population of the City of Glasgow was around 580,000 in the 2001 census, with about 1.2 million living in the Greater Glasgow area.

Since the early 2000s, the city's financial services industry has grown, with many of the world's financial services companies opening offices in the area known as "Wall Street on Clyde".

# PUBLIC TRANSPORT HISTORY

Glasgow had one of the largest tramway systems in Europe, which at its maximum comprised over 1200 trams, covering 141 route miles (227km) within the city and beyond. The size, and geographical coverage of the system, warrants a separate publication, but the main historical points are outlined below in order to give some background to the eventual introduction of trolleybuses.

The first horse drawn omnibuses appeared in the city from 1845, and the operators' fleets grew to provide frequent services for the citizens. However the interest in railed street public transport gained momentum in the second half of the century, with many horse drawn tramways being commissioned throughout the UK.

The Glasgow Street Tramways Act of 1870 allowed the Corporation to build tramways, but stipulated they must be leased to a private operating company for 22 years. The first horse drawn tram opened the system on 19th August 1872 between St George's Cross and Eglinton Toll, the operator being The Glasgow Tramway and Omnibus Company. At the end of the 22 year period the lease was not renewed, and Glasgow Corporation Tramways took over the operation from 1st July 1894.

The use of electric traction began on 13th October 1898, initially using trolley pole current collection, but with a change to the bow collectors in the early 1930s; the latter were to have an adverse impact when trolleybuses were introduced.

The electric tram fleet grew quickly in the first half of the 20th century, with the majority being produced at the Corporation's Coplawhill Workshops, and with electrical power supplied from the city's Pinkston Power Station from 1901. "Standard" cars were produced in large numbers between 1898 and 1924, many receiving subsequent modernisation. The Airdrie and Coatbridge, plus the Paisley District tramway companies was purchased in 1922/23. Trolleybuses were first considered in the early 1920s to provide feeder services to the tramway, but not progressed.

Streamlined "Coronation" cars were introduced in the late 1930s, plus a further six in 1954. Post the Second World War saw the introduction of "Cunarder" cars, which were an updated version of the pre-war "Coronation" design, and they were the last completely new double deck trams to be built in the UK. In addition, a number of "Green Goddess" trams were purchased from Liverpool Corporation in 1954.

The tramway system was gradually phased out between 1949 and 1962, with a final official closure date of 4th September 1962, trams being replaced predominantly by motorbuses, plus a much smaller trolleybus fleet, which is the subject of this album.

The publication of the Glasgow Corporation Provisional Order in 1933 sought to operate trolleybuses over tramway routes, which resulted in vigorous opposition from bus and rail companies at the Public Enquiry. Approval was given, but with restrictions, including the inability to build trolleybuses, with adverse employment implications for the Coplawhill Workshops. As a result, there was no action before the outbreak of war in 1939, although in 1937 consideration was given to the use of a hybrid diesel-electric vehicle, but this was not pursued.

After the Second World War, the city had a large ageing tram fleet, where the track and vehicle maintenance had suffered during the war years, notwithstanding the introduction of the 100 modern "Cunarder" cars between 1948 and 1952, and the 46 second hand vehicles from Liverpool in 1954. Extension of the tramway system into post war housing estates and industrial areas would have resulted in unaffordable capital costs, so it was decided in 1945 to experiment with trolleybuses. There had been much pre-war opposition to the use of this type of vehicle because of the reduction of manpower at the Coplawhill Workshops, and amongst track maintenance staff. Nevertheless, the use of trolleybuses would continue to provide generating load for the Pinkston Power Station, which used locally produced coal. The power station continued to be owned by the Corporation up to 1958, whereas the rest of the electricity generation industry had been nationalised by the Labour Government in the late 1940s.

Because the trams used bow current collection they could not use the dual trolleybus overhead wiring and, where the two crossed, special insulated fittings had to be used, leaving the trolleybuses traversing long dead electrical sections. These problems led to trams and trolleybuses being segregated as far as possible, particularly in narrow streets, with the trolleybus route development being drastically constrained as a result.

Orders were placed for 20 three-axle trolleybuses, 12 AEC and 8 Daimler, whose bodies by MCCW were to have had rear platform entrance doors and front sliding door exits. However, in order to expedite early delivery Glasgow agreed to accept, as did Newcastle Corporation, identical bodies that MCCW was building for London Transport's Q1 trolleybuses, and in 1947 the order was increased to 34 BUTs (AEC and Leyland having combined their trolleybus activities as British United Traction), and 30 Daimlers, all fitted with the London style bodies.

The first trolleybus service was 102 between Polmadie and Riddrie, which commenced on 3nd April 1949, replacing tram Service 2; initially motorbuses helped out until trolleybus deliveries improved. On 3rd July 1949, the service was extended from Polmadie to Hampden Park. When Service 103 was introduced between Riddrie and Hampden Park in August 1950, the 102 was cut back to Polmadie; however vehicles returning from Hampden Park on Service 103 displayed 102.

On 6th November 1949, Service 101 was introduced, initially with motorbus help, between Cathedral Street and Shawfield, partially replacing tram Service 10, and on 6th August 1950 the service was extended from Cathedral Street to Royston Road, part way along the route to Riddrie.

Initially the trolleybuses for these services were temporally housed at Larkfield Garage, but from 17th December 1950 they were transferred to the newly opened Hampden Garage, which had been specially built for trolleybuses.

On 5th March 1951, a single deck BUT "standee" trolleybus made its first appearance, which included limited seating, but with space for forty standing passengers. It incorporated a front exit, and a rear entrance, where there was a circulating area for waiting passengers to pass a seated conductor. The following year an order was placed for ten more, but with a widened exit door positioned behind the front axle. The vehicles were not entirely successful, and were later modified to a single entrance/exit, with seating replacing much of the standing area and the conductor's desk.

From 31st August 1952, Service 104 opened from Cathedral Street to Muirend, replacing parts of motorbus Service 37. From 5th July 1953, part of tram Service 13 was converted to trolleybus operation as Service 105 from Queen's Cross to Clarkston, the only service, together with Service 107 (see later), to cross the city centre, and twenty 2-axle Sunbeams were added to the fleet. From 19th February 1956, the 101 service was extended from Shawfield to Rutherglen, having been temporally operated by motorbuses for the previous six months.

The motorbus night service between George Square and Clarkston was replaced by trolleybuses from 16th December 1956 as a result of the Suez crisis, with the former resuming on 27th November 1960. On 7th July 1957 Service 107 opened between Maitland Street and Muirend via Victoria Road replacing parts of motorbus Services 18 and 43, and operated by the first vehicles from the delivery of 90 two-axle BUT trolleybuses. The following year the long east/ west tram Service 7 between Millerston/Riddrie and Bellahouston was converted to trolleybus operation from 15th June 1958 as Service 106.

The final tram to trolleybus conversion came later in the year, the last in the UK, when the suburban tram Service 12 between Mount Florida (Hampden Park) and Paisley Road Toll became Service 108 on 15th November 1958. There was a further experiment with single deck vehicles for this service, which required special Ministry of Transport dispensation for their manufacture to a 34.5ft (10.5m) length. Ten were ordered using a BUT export chassis specification and fitted with fifty seat bodies. Again, these were not entirely successful in service, with delays stemming from the front single narrow entrance/exit doorway. Also from 15th November 1958 both Services 106 and 108 were extended to the Linthouse and Shieldhall areas to provide workmen's services for the neighbouring shipyards and associated industries.

It is perhaps significant that earlier in 1958 the Corporation agreed that all remaining trams would be replaced by motorbuses, with trolleybuses being restricted to a maximum fleet of 200. The cost of replacing trams with trolleybuses would have been £2 million more than motorbuses, and in addition, the Corporation agreed to sell the Pinkston Power Station to the South of Scotland Electricity Board, which would provide over £1 million, but with the loss of determining traction charges for its fleets.

The increase in car ownership, and changes to the areas that trolleybuses served, led to a gradual reduction in services. The southern section of Service 103/102 between Polmadie and Hampden Park was withdrawn on 9th May 1959, peak hour services generally reduced in 1961, and Service 104 between Cathedral Street and Muirend finished on 6th January 1962, after trying to make the service more economic by the use of off peak single deck vehicles.

On 2nd September 1962, the northern termini of Services 101 and 102 were reversed, with 101 being extended from Royston Road to Riddrie, and 102 cut back to Royston Road, involving a substantial reduction in the frequency of the latter.

In the financial year ending May 1962, trolleybuses made a loss of £88,000 attributed, in the main, to the higher cost of electricity from the new supplier. Workmen's services of the extended 106 and 108 to Linthouse and Shieldhall were replaced by motorbuses from 15th November 1964, with consequent reduction in the trolleybus fleet.

From 28th February 1965, Sunday services were withdrawn on the 107, and in January 1966 it was announced that all trolleybuses would be withdrawn and replaced by motorbuses. First to go were Services 101 and 102 on 30th April 1966, followed by Service 106 on 1st October of the same year.

1967 saw the last three services cease trolleybus operation, namely 107 and 108 on 4th March, and finally the long 105 provided the last service trolleybus on 27th May 1967. However, TB123 made an appearance the next day, initially under battery power with booms raised, but to everyone's surprise moved under power along Aikenhead Road, before being towed away from Gorbals Cross.

Thus ended 18 years of trolleybus operation in the city, and when including trams, totalled nearly 69 years of electrically powered street public transport.

## Service Numbers as at January 1959

| | |
|---|---|
| 101 | Royston Road - Shawfield/Rutherglen |
| 102 | Riddrie - Polmadie |
| 103 | Riddrie - Hampden Park (return as 102) |
| 104 | Cathedral Street - Muirend |
| 105 | Queen's Cross - Mount Florida/ Muirend/Clarkston |
| 106 | Millerston/Riddrie - Bellahouston (extended to Linthouse/Shieldhall for peak workmen services) |
| 107 | Maitland Street - Muirend |
| 108 | Mount Florida - Paisley Road Toll (extended to Linthouse/Shieldhall for peak workmen services) |
| 5 | George Square - Clarkston (Night Service) |

## Abbreviations

| | |
|---|---|
| AEC | Associated Equipment Company (bus and trolleybus chassis) |
| BRS | British Road Services |
| BUT | British United Traction (trolleybus chassis) |
| LNER | London and North Eastern Railway |
| LMSR | London Midland and Scottish Railway |
| MCCW | Metropolitan - Cammell Carriage and Waggon (bodywork) |
| NTA | National Trolleybus Association |
| PTE | Passenger Transport Executive |
| SMT | Scottish Motor Traction |
| STMS | Scottish Tramway Museum Society |
| TSB | Trustee Savings Bank |
| UK | United Kingdom |

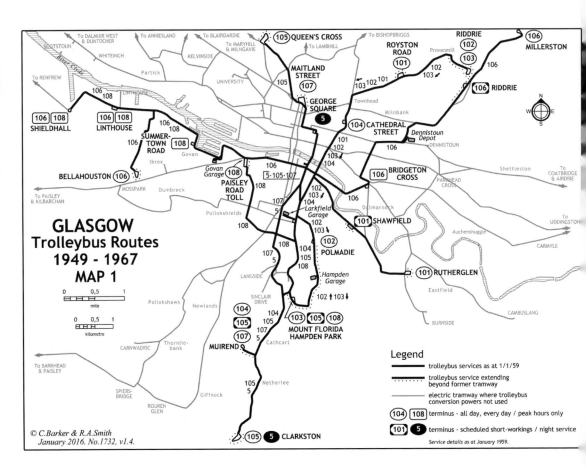

**GLASGOW**
**Trolleybus Routes**
**1949 - 1967**
**MAP 1**

Legend

| | |
|---|---|
| ▬▬▬ | trolleybus services as at 1/1/59 |
| ▬▬▬ | trolleybus service extending beyond former tramway |
| ▬▬▬ | electric tramway where trolleybus conversion powers not used |
| (104) (108) | terminus - all day, every day / peak hours only |
| (101) 5 | terminus - scheduled short-workings / night service |

© C.Barker & R.A.Smith
January 2016. No.1732, v1.4.

Service details as at January 1959.

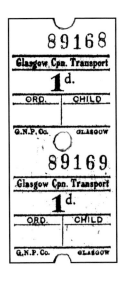

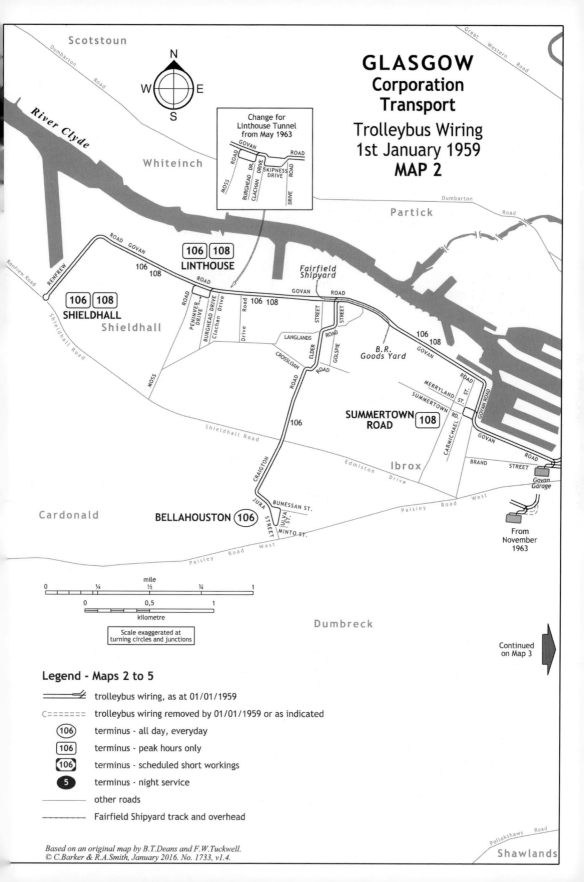

# GLASGOW
## Corporation Transport
### Trolleybus Wiring 1st January 1959
### MAP 2

Scotstoun

N
W E
S

River Clyde

Whiteinch

Partick

Change for
Linthouse Tunnel
from May 1963

GOVAN
ROAD     ROAD
MOSS ROAD
BURGHEAD DR.
CLACHAN DRIVE
SKIPNESS DRIVE
DRIVE

Dumbarton    Road

[106] [108]
LINTHOUSE

106
108

ROAD GOVAN

Fairfield
Shipyard

GOVAN    ROAD

[106] [108]
SHIELDHALL

Shieldhall

Renfrew Road
RENFREW

Shieldhall Road

PENINVER DRIVE
BURGHEAD DRIVE
CLACHAN DRIVE
DRIVE

106 108

GOVAN    ROAD

LANGLANDS    ROAD

CROSSLOAN
ROAD
ELDER
ROAD
GOLSPIE
STREET
ELDER
STREET
GOLSPIE
STREET

MOSS

Shieldhall Road

106

B.R.
Goods Yard

106
108

GOVAN

MERRYLAND    ST.
SUMMERTOWN    RD.
CARMICHAEL    ST.
GOVAN ROAD

SUMMERTOWN
ROAD    [108]

GOVAN
ROAD

Cardonald

CRAIGTON STREET
JURA STREET
BUNESSAN ST.
ULVA ST.
MINTO ST.

BELLAHOUSTON (106)

Edmiston    Drive

Ibrox

BRAND    STREET

Govan
Garage

Paisley    Road    West

From
November
1963

Paisley    Road    West

Dumbreck

Continued
on Map 3

mile
0    ¼    ½    ¾    1

0    0,5    1
kilometre

Scale exaggerated at
turning circles and junctions

Pollokshaws    Road

Shawlands

## Legend - Maps 2 to 5

trolleybus wiring, as at 01/01/1959

C======= trolleybus wiring removed by 01/01/1959 or as indicated

(106) terminus - all day, everyday

[106] terminus - peak hours only

(106) terminus - scheduled short workings

(5) terminus - night service

——— other roads

·········· Fairfield Shipyard track and overhead

Based on an original map by B.T.Deans and F.W.Tuckwell.
© C.Barker & R.A.Smith, January 2016. No. 1733, v1.4.

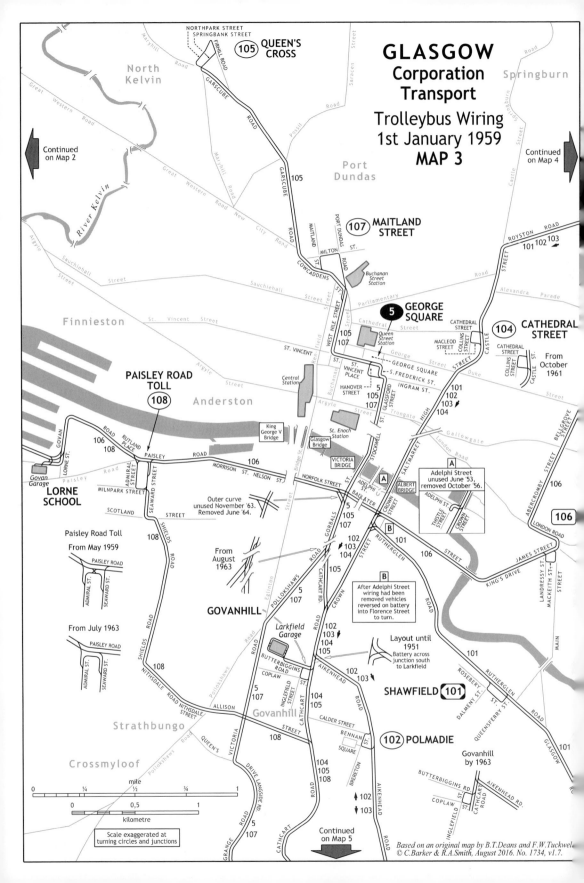

# GLASGOW
## Corporation Transport
### Trolleybus Wiring
### 1st January 1959
### MAP 3

Continued on Map 2

Continued on Map 4

NORTHPARK STREET
SPRINGBANK STREET

(105) QUEEN'S CROSS

North Kelvin

Springburn

Port Dundas

(107) MAITLAND STREET

101 102 103

Buchanan Street Station

(5) GEORGE SQUARE

Finnieston

Queen Street Station

(104) CATHEDRAL STREET

From October 1961

MACLEOD STREET
COLLINS STREET

CATHEDRAL STREET
COLLINS STREET
CASTLE ST.

PAISLEY ROAD TOLL

(108)

Anderston

King George V Bridge

Central Station

HANOVER STREET

St. Enoch Station

Glasgow Bridge

VICTORIA BRIDGE

Govan Garage

LORNE SCHOOL

106 108

MORRISON ST. NELSON ST.

NORFOLK STREET

MILNPARK STREET

SCOTLAND STREET

Outer curve unused November '63. Removed June '64.

Paisley Road Toll
From May 1959

PAISLEY ROAD

ADMIRAL ST.
SEAWARD ST.

From August 1963

From July 1963

PAISLEY ROAD

ADMIRAL ST.
SEAWARD ST.

GOVANHILL

Larkfield Garage

BUTTERBIGGINS ROAD

COPLAW
INGLEFIELD STREET

Govanhill

Strathbungo

Crossmyloof

[A] Adelphi Street unused June '53, removed October '56.

ADELPHI ST.
THISTLE STREET
CROWN STREET

ALBERT BRIDGE

[B] After Adelphi Street wiring had been removed vehicles reversed on battery into Florence Street to turn.

Layout until 1951
Battery across junction south to Larkfield

SHAWFIELD (101)

(102) POLMADIE

Govanhill by 1963

BUTTERBIGGINS RD.
AIKENHEAD RD.
COPLAW ST.
CATHCART ROAD
INGLEFIELD ST.

(106)

BENNAN SQUARE

BRERETON

CALDER STREET

ROSEBERY ST.
DALMENY ST.
QUEENSFERRY ST.

KING'S DRIVE

RUTHERGLEN ROAD

GLASGOW ROAD

MAIN

LANDRESSY ST.
MACKEITH ST.

JAMES STREET

0    ¼    mile    ½    ¾    1

0    0,5    kilometre    1

Scale exaggerated at turning circles and junctions

Continued on Map 5

*Based on an original map by B.T.Deans and F.W.Tuckwell*
© C.Barker & R.A.Smith, August 2016. No. 1734, v1.7.

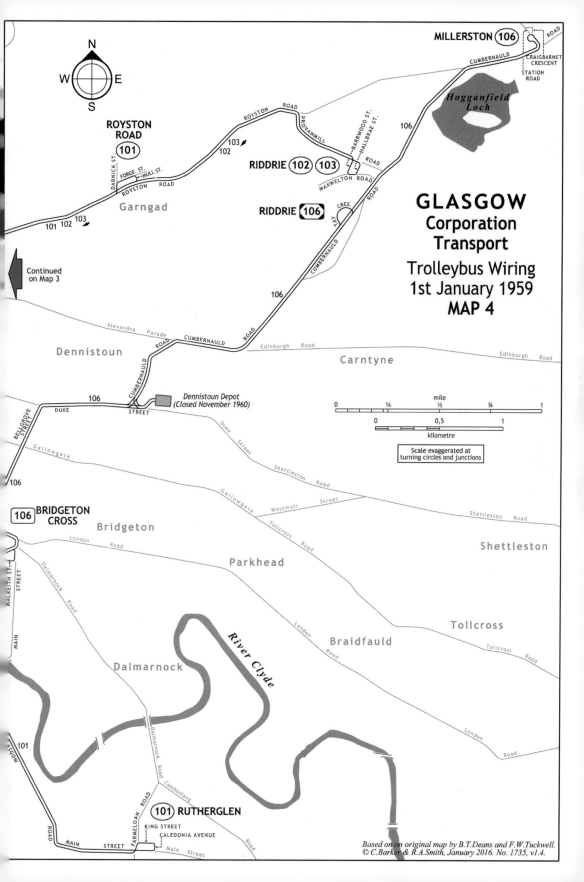

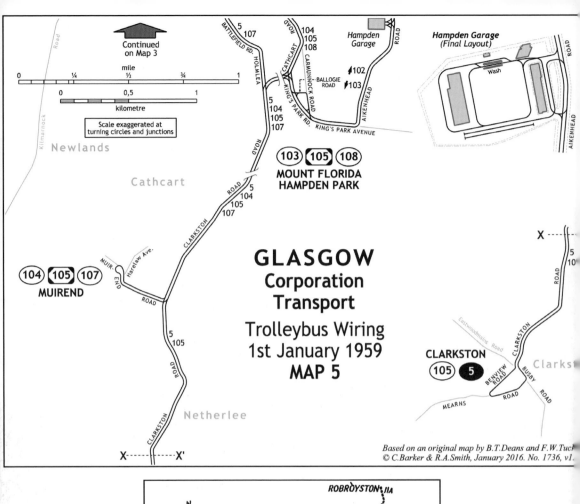

GLASGOW
Corporation
Transport
Trolleybus Wiring
1st January 1959
MAP 5

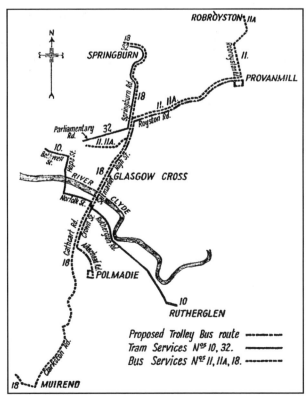

# RIDDRIE TO CATHEDRAL STREET
## (SERVICES 101/102/103)

1.   The Riddrie terminus was a "round the houses" loop from Provanmill Road into Barrwood Street, where we see BUT TB25 on Service 101 to Rutherglen.  It has just passed under a section insulator, before entering Maxwelton Road where the layover will be taken; return to Provanmill Road was via Hallbrae Street. A second vehicle follows close behind, and the overhead wiring curve into the loop can be seen in the distance.  The 101 service originally ran between Cathedral Street and Shawfield from November 1949, before being extended north to Royston Road in August 1950, and subsequently to Riddrie in September 1962.  At the southern end, the service was extended from Shawfield to Rutherglen in February 1956. (Travel Lens Photographic)

2.   BUT TB4 waits at the terminal stand in Maxwelton Road, amongst local authority housing stock, before returning to Polmadie on Service 102, which opened in April 1949, and extended to Hampden Park in July 1949.  When Service 103 was introduced between Hampden Park and Riddrie in August 1950, the 102 was cut back to its original terminus at Polmadie; however, vehicles returning north from Hampden Park displayed Service 102.  Note the pre-fabricated bungalows (prefabs) on the left, which were erected to overcome the immediate housing shortage after the Second World War. They no longer exist, as the land they stand on forms the boundary of the M8 Motorway.  (P Mitchell)

3.  The Royston Road terminal loop was used as a short working for Service 102 and became its terminus after the cut back from Riddrie in September 1962; at the same time Service 101 was extended from here to Riddrie.  BUT TB13 waits at the Darnick Street stand before returning to Polmadie in the above month.  To reach this point vehicles left Royston Road, and travelled round the loop via Mull and Forge Streets.  The four storey tenements have made way for modern semi-detached housing, although there is still a single storey "Glen Bar" on the corner.  (C Routh)

4.  Having travelled the length of Royston Road towards the city, Sunbeam TG15 is about to turn into Castle Street on Service 101 to Shawfield, with a second trolleybuses to the rear.  The buildings beyond have disappeared, and the whole area is now the floodlit sports ground of St Roch's Secondary School.  (P Mitchell)

5.   BUT TB31 turns out of Castle Street into Royston Road, almost opposite the previous picture, en route to Riddrie.  Under the overbridge that TB31 has just crossed was the Monkland Canal on the left, leading to the St Rollox Basin on the right.  The canal was constructed to bring coal from the Monklands into Glasgow, and was connected to the Forth and Clyde Canal; much of the former's alignment is now under the M8 Motorway.  All the buildings have gone, but a Cadburys Whole Nut Chocolate Bar can still be purchased, but not for 6d (2.5p). (R F Mack/S Fozard copyright)

6.   BUT TB3 has travelled down Castle Street, destined for Rutherglen on Service 101, and is about to pass Monkland Street.  The St Rollox branch of the Glasgow Savings Bank is on the left; this organisation became part of the TSB Bank Scotland, eventually merging with Lloyds Bank. The buildings have disappeared under Junction 15 of the M8 Motorway.  The following car is a Standard 10. (R F Mack/NTA)

# CATHEDRAL STREET TO ALBERT BRIDGE
## (SERVICES 101/102/103/104)

7. The Cathedral Street loop provided a short working facility for northbound Services 101/102/103, and was the terminus for Service 104 to Muirend. Originally, vehicles travelled clockwise around Macleod, Collins and Cathedral Streets, but the direction was reversed from October 1961. Sunbeam TG6 waits to travel south to Shawfield on Service 101. Note that in all the pictures so far vehicles have had their "via" destination panel painted over, which was an economy measure implemented in around 1958. Two years earlier, the complete rear destination display on early vehicles was covered. (S Lockwood collection)

8. In the early days of the system, BUT TB1, complete with London Passenger Transport Board style roundels, original cream roof and full destination display, is seen in Crown Street destined for the original northern terminus of Service 101 in Cathedral Street, before the extension to Royston Road. The London roundels were soon removed. The advertisement is for a well known Glasgow bakery. (C Carter)

9.   Two vehicles from the original 1949/50 delivery of trolleybuses for the opening services are depicted.  Both are travelling south along High Street, with BUT TB23 in the foreground on Service 101 to Rutherglen, followed by Daimler TD16 destined for Polmadie on Service 102; although they appear identical, the BUTs could be identified by the rear wheel chrome hubs.  Behind the motorbus is High Street Station, and the building on the right was part of the LMSR College Goods Station.  To the north of High Street Station was the LNER High Street Goods Station. (R F Mack/NTA)

10.   Daimler TD26 travels south along High Street adjacent to Bell Street, and approaches the Glasgow Cross stop on Service 104 to Muirend.  The vehicle is devoid of advertisements, and carries a full destination display.  Glasgow trolleybus blinds had white lettering on a green background, although from 1963 many received the more usual white characters on black.  Apart from shop names, little has changed to this scene at the time of writing. (C Routh)

11. This scene at Glasgow Cross, where five roads cross, depicts BUT TB30 leaving High Street to enter Saltmarket on Service 102 to Polmadie, closely followed by a second vehicle on Service 101 to Shawfield or Rutherglen. Until the early 1960s, trams crossed at 90 degrees, as indicated by the single overhead wires above the rear vehicle. In the distance is a Glasgow Daimler motorbus. (R F Mack/S Fozard copyright)

12. A rather battered BUT TBS2 is seen at the same location, with the base of the Tolbooth Steeple on the left. The latter dates from 1625/26, and was earlier connected a former building on the left. The single decker was the first of the batch with the exit door behind the front axle, and is on Service 103 to Hampden Park. All the batch were subsequently altered to single doorway, with conductor's desk removed, thereby providing increased seating capacity. The tram overhead wiring referred to in the previous picture can be seen more clearly in this view, and TBS2 is followed by a Bedford lorry owned by haulage contractor John F Dunn Ltd. (R Brook/P Watson)

13.   Also at the same location, the linesmen aloft on Bedford tower wagon FGG 596 are carrying out emergency repair work where the tram overhead crosses the trolleybus wiring.  An Inspector stands in front of Daimler TD16, which is waiting to move from High Street into Saltmarket on Service 101 to Rutherglen.  In the right background is a replica of the original Mercat (Market) Cross, which is an octagonal tower built in 1929, with a heraldic unicorn on top.  On the left is Central SMT Bristol Lodekka B38, closely followed by a Hillman Minx car.
(V Nutton/Travel Lens Photographic)

14.   This view provides a good side elevation of Daimler TD22 in Saltmarket outside the Old Ship Bank Vaults, site of the Old Ship Bank, which was the city's first bank. The bank subsequently moved, with the site becoming a public house in the mid 19th century. This was rebuilt in 1904. Adjacent to the top of the traction standard on the left is a wall rosette, which supported tramway overhead wiring. (C Carter)

15. BUT TB65, on Service 102 to Polmadie, is about to leave Saltmarket and cross Albert Bridge to enter Crown Street; on the left is the original High Court of Justiciary building. A Caledonian articulated lorry passes on the left; the company operated out of Dumfries in the 1950s/60s and early 1970s, eventually becoming part of Scottish Road Services (SRS) of Galashiels. (Travel Lens Photographic)

16. We now reach the Albert Bridge across the River Clyde, with tram track still in place, although their overhead wiring has been removed. BUT TB14, with London Transport style roundels and complete destination display, crosses the bridge on Service 101 to Shawfield. The bridge was opened in 1871, and named after Queen Victoria's consort, being the fifth bridge to be built on the site; it has recently received a multimillion pound restoration. (C Carter)

# OUTWARDS TO SHAWFIELD AND RUTHERGLEN
## (SERVICE 101)

17.  Having crossed Albert Bridge, BUT TB1 has just left Crown Street and entered Rutherglen Road circa 1960/61; it is just about to pass under a section insulator.  These were required every half mile, so that an electrical failure in one section did not affect those either side; it was usually where electricity was fed into the overhead, but not in this case.  Visual indication of a section insulator was the white band painted on the traction standards, warning the driver to coast (not take power) under the insulated fitting.  The buildings in view will soon disappear, as the tall crane in the background assists with the construction of the twenty storey Hutchesontown C twin tower blocks. They were built in a stark "Brutalist" style of architecture, and were demolished in 1993 following major problems with damp and infestations.  (P Mitchell)

| Stage No. | | | | | | | | | | | Trolleybus Service No. 101<br>RUTHERGLEN or SHAWFIELD and RIDDRIE<br>No Weekly Tickets |
|---|---|---|---|---|---|---|---|---|---|---|---|
| 24 | | | | | | | | | | | Rutherglen (King Street at Farmeloan Road) |
| 25 | 3 | | | | | | | | | | White's Works |
| 26 | 4 | 3 | | | | | | | | | Shawfield |
| 27 | 6 | 4 | 3 | | | | | | | | Braehead Street |
| 28 | 6 | 6 | 4 | 3 | | | | | | | Crown Street, 129 |
| 29 | 9 | 6 | 6 | 4 | 3 | | | | | | Glasgow Cross |
| 30 | 9 | 9 | 6 | 6 | 4 | 3 | | | | | Cathedral Street or Duke Street |
| 31 | 10 | 9 | 9 | 6 | 6 | 4 | 3 | | | | Castle Street at Parliamentary Rd |
| 32 | 10 | 10 | 9 | 9 | 6 | 6 | 4 | 3 | | | Tharsis Street |
| 33 | 1s | 10 | 10 | 9 | 9 | 6 | 6 | 4 | 3 | | Royston Road, 617 |
| 34 | 1s | 1s | 10 | 10 | 9 | 9 | 6 | 6 | 4 | 3 | Provanmill Road at Royston Road |
| 35 | 1s | 1s | 1s | 10 | 10 | 9 | 9 | 6 | 6 | 4 | 3 | Riddrie (Maxwelton Rd) |

Fare Chart (July 1964)

18. "Standee" BUT TBS10 has reached the Shawfield terminal stand in Queensferry Street before returning to Royston Road via Rosebery and Dalmeny Streets. Originally, the return journey would have terminated at Cathedral Street, before being extended to Royston Road in August 1950; Service 101 was extended from Shawfield to Rutherglen in February 1956. TBS10 is in original livery and two door format, whilst the lone dog looks towards tenement buildings that, despite subsequent modernisation, no longer exist. (P Mitchell)

19. With Shawfield Stadium as a backdrop, Sunbeam TG3 leaves Rutherglen Road and enters Glasgow Road en route to Rutherglen; the Shawfield terminus is a little way to the rear at the city boundary. The stadium was the home of Clyde Football Club until 1986, before settling in Cumbernauld, and the Glasgow Tigers speedway team made it their base for a decade in the 1980/90s. The stadium still provides greyhound racing twice a week. The road on the right, beyond the BP sign, was the site of the Shawfield Service 18A tram terminus.
(R F Mack/S Fozard copyright)

20.  BUT TB1 travels along Glasgow Road towards Rutherglen, between the factory fencing of J & J White's chemical works (later ACC Chrome and Chemicals), having passed under the bridge, which was the site that originally gave access to works railway sidings from the ex-Caledonian/ LMSR line at Polmadie.  The company produced chromate products, leaving the site contaminated with toxic waste.  The intermediate destination panel of TB1 has been painted out, and Shawfield Stadium can be seen in the far distance.  (Author's collection)

21.  BUT TB17 has just left Glasgow Road on the run up from Shawfield, and entered the western end of Rutherglen Main Street.  Greenbank Street is on the right, which has been shortened further back, with the section depicted on the right now named Victoria Place.  The section where TB17 is seen is now a service road (King Street) running parallel with Main Street.  (P Mitchell)

22.    The imposing tower of the Grade A listed Rutherglen Town Hall, which is now used for weddings, plus social and cultural events, forms the backdrop for BUT TBS7 as it makes its way along Main Street on the last leg of the journey to the Rutherglen terminus.  It is painted in the later simplified livery, and is just about to pass under a section insulator, again identified by the white area on the traction standard.  Compare this with Picture 17, as on this occasion electrical power is being fed to the overhead wiring from the local substation in King Street.  (P Mitchell)

23.    BUT TB29, on a short working to Cathedral Street, leaves the Rutherglen terminal loop to re-join Main Street.  This last leg was along Farmeloan Road, which was still served by tram Services 18 and 26 as illustrated by the track and single overhead wires.  Where trolleybus wiring crossed that for trams, drivers of the former had to coast through long "dead sections" which avoided the tram's bow collector coming into contact with the negative trolleybus wire; an example can be seen adjacent to the peak of the church gable end.  The newsagent on the right was the local booking agent for the Central SMT bus company, and all the buildings either side of the Rutherglen East Parish Church tower have disappeared, to be replaced by a modern office complex.  (P Mitchell)

24.  At the Rutherglen terminal stand in King Street, Daimler TD17 waits before making a return trip to Royston Road.  To reach King Street, TD17 left Main Street, and travelled along Caledonia Avenue; on departure it will join Farmeloan Road.  Looking to the advertisement, the need for Kodak roll film has greatly reduced in this digital age, although it can still be obtained.  The building on the left is the local police station.  (P Mitchell)

## 101 — RIDDRIE to SHAWFIELD or R'GLEN

| Week-days a.m. | a.m. | p.m. | p.m. | a.m. | p.m. | p.m. |
|---|---|---|---|---|---|---|
| | 8 46† | 4 3* | 6 51 | 10 46 | 6 7 | 11 45† |
| 5 20* | 50* | 8 | 58* | 51* | 13* | 55† |
| 34* | 54† | 18* | 7 6 | 56* | 14† | 12 4† |
| 54 | 57† | 23 | 7½ ms | 11 1 | 19 | |
| 6 4 | 9 1 | 28* | Alt. | | 6* | 25* Suns. |
| 16 | 9* | 33* | Shaw | 11* | 26† | a.m. |
| 28 | 20 | 36 | R'glen | 16 | 31 | 6 48* |
| 40 | 9 30* | 39* | 11 6 | 21* | 37* | 7 2* |
| 48 | 10 ms | 45* | 13* | 26* | 43 | 31* |
| 53 | Alt. | 48 | 21* | 31 | 49* | 8 0* |
| 57* | R'glen | 54* | 28* | 35* | 55 | 8 20 |
| 7 1 | Shaw | 5 0 | 34† | 43 | 7 1* | 20 ms |
| 5* | 11 20 | 6* | 41† | 47* | 7 | p.m. |
| 9 | 30* | 9* | 49† | 51* | 13* | 12 40 |
| 12* | 42* | 12 | 56† | 55 | 19 | 55 |
| 16 | 54* | 15* | 12 4† | 59* | 25* | 1 7 |
| 20* | p.m. | 18* | Sats. | 31* | 15* | |
| 24 | 12 0 | 21* | a.m. | 12 3* | 37 | 22 |
| 27* | 12 6* | 24 | 5 20* | 7 | 44* | 30* |
| 31 | 6 ms | 27* | 34* | 11* | 52 | 37 |
| 35* | Alt. | 30* | 54 | 15* | 59* | 45* |
| 39 | R'glen | 33* | 6 4 | 19 | 8 0† | 52 |
| 42* | Shaw | 36 | 16 | 23* | 7 | 2 0* |
| 46 | 1 42* | 39* | 30 | 27* | 14* | 2 7 |
| 50* | 48† | 42* | 45 | 31 | 22 | Same |
| 54 | 54 | 45* | 7 1 | 35* | 8 29* | Each |
| 57* | 2 0* | 48† | 8* | 39* | 7½ ms | hour |
| 8 1 | 8 | 51 | 7 16 | 43 | Alt. | till |
| 5* | 15* | 54† | 7½ ms | 47* | Shaw | 10 52 |
| 9 | 23 | 57* | R'glen | 51* | R'glen | 58* |
| 12* | 26† | 6 0† | Shaw | 55 | 9 52 | 11 4 |
| 16 | 30* | 3† | 10 1 | 59* | 58* | 12* |
| 20* | 38 | 6 | 6* | 1 3* | 10 4 | 19 |
| 24 | 2 45* | 9† | 11* | Same | 6 ms | 28 |
| 27† | 7½ ms | 12* | 16 | each | Alt. | 34† |
| 31† | Alt. | 15† | 21* | hour | Shaw | 49† |
| 31† | R'glen | 24 | 26* | till | R'glen | 12 4† |
| 35* | Shaw | 30* | 31 | 5 55 | 11 28 | |
| 39† | 3 45* | 38 | 36* | 6 1* | 33† | |
| 42 | 53 | 43* | 41* | 2† | 39† | |

* To Shawfield   † To Hampden Gar.

## 101 — RUTHERGLEN to RIDDRIE

| Week-days a.m. | a.m. | p.m. | Sats. a.m. | p.m. | p.m. | p.m. |
|---|---|---|---|---|---|---|
| | 8 48† | 2 32 | | 7 31 | 11 51† | 15 ms |
| 6 30 | 54 | 15 ms | 6 30 | 15 ms | 12 3† | 11 30 |
| 41 | 9 4 | 4 2 | 41 | 9 1 | | 38† |
| 51 | 20 ms | 18 | 54 | 20 | | 53† |
| 7 3 | 11 24 | 4 36 | 7 9 | 38 | Suns. | 12 2† |
| 10 | 42 | 12 ms | 15 ms | 9 52 | a.m. | |
| 7 18 | p.m. | 6 0 | 11 39 | 12 ms | 6 15 | |
| 7½ ms | 12 0 | 15 ms | 55 | 11 4 | 9 0 | |
| 8 33 | 12 ms | 11 30 | p.m. | 20 | 20 ms | |
| 40† | 2 0 | 40† | 12 2† | 29 | 1 0 | |
| | 17 | 12 2† | 12 ms | 39† | | |

## 101 — SHAWFIELD to RIDDRIE

| Week-days a.m. | a.m. | p.m. | Sats. a.m. | a.m. | p.m. | p.m. |
|---|---|---|---|---|---|---|
| | 11 20 | 5 3 | 10 55 | 12 57 | 11 51† | |
| 5 0 | 42 | 9 | 5 0 | 11 5 | 1 5 | |
| 15 | p.m. | 15 | 12 | 10 | Same | |
| 30 | 12 0 | 21 | 30 | †20 | each | Suns. |
| 48 | 12 12 | 24 | 48 | †25 | hour | a.m. |
| 6 0 | 12 ms | 27 | 6 0 | †41 | till | 6 35 |
| 12 | 2 0 | 33 | 15 | 5 57 | 7 0 | |
| 24 | 2 15 | 36 | 30 | 7 | 20 | |
| 41 | 15 ms | †39 | 54 | 12 ms | 40 | |
| 54 | 4 0 | 45 | 15 ms | 7 31 | 8 0 | |
| 7 1 | 4 | 6 0 | 12 5 | 7 44 | 27 | |
| 5 | 15 | 6 13 | 9 | 15 ms | 46 | |
| 12 | 18 | 15 ms | 10 | 9 14 | p.m. | |
| 7 20 | 30 | 11 28 | 20 | 32 | 12 59 | |
| 7½ ms | 36 | 41† | 25 | 9 52 | 10 59 | |
| 8 50 | 47† | 49† | 35 | 11 16 | 11 13† | |
| 9 5† | 48 | | 41 | 27† | 26† | |
| 9 20 | 5 0 | | 53 | 39† | 40† | |

‡ To Cathedral St.   † To Hampden Gar.

| Riddrie to Castle St. | .. | .. | 11 mins. |
|---|---|---|---|
| Castle St. to Glasgow Cross | .. | .. | 7 ,, |
| Glasgow Cross to Shawfield | .. | .. | 10 ,, |
| Glasgow Cross to Rutherglen | .. | .. | 16 ,, |

Timetable (November 1962)

25.   Having left Albert Bridge, and the junction with Rutherglen Road, BUT TBS5 travels south along Crown Street on Service 102 to Polmadie, with Cumberland Street on the left. The vehicle has been modified with only a single entrance/exit.  An Albion lorry of Gray Dunn, a local biscuit maker, follows as a Hillman Minx travels in the opposite direction; the seated dog seems oblivious to passing traffic.  The area beyond the Hillman car has made way for a multi-storey apartment building.  (R F Mack/NTA)

26.   BUT TB4 travels south along the northern end of Cathcart Road, and will shortly turn left into Aikenhead Road, and onwards on Service 102 to Polmadie.  In the distance stands the St Ninian's Wynd Church at the junction with Crown Street, where two trolleybuses on Service 105 can be seen; TB4 is roughly where the current M74 passes under the road.  The sign board immediately above the Land Rover indi-cates that the com-pany were boiler scalers and ship rig-gers, providing an illustration of Glas-gow's lost shipping industry. First Glas-gow's Caledonia bus garage, the largest in Scotland, now occu-pies the site. (P Mitchell)

27.  The tenement buildings, none of which exist today, tower above BUT TB21 as it makes its way along Aikenhead Road near Batson Street, having turned out of Cathcart Road in the distance. Although destined for Polmadie on Service 102, the destination blind shows the return journey to Royston Road.  Note the single example of X style catenary suspension carrying the overhead wiring, which was installed to examine whether span wires could be replaced while power was on in daylight hours.  Nottingham used similar suspension, but on a more widespread basis, on parts of their system in the early years.  There were also early examples in Huddersfield.  (P Mitchell)

**Trolleybus Service No. 102**

**ROYSTON ROAD and POLMADIE**

**No Weekly Tickets**

| Stage No. | | | | | | | | |
|---|---|---|---|---|---|---|---|---|
| 33 | Royston Road (at Darnick Street) | | | | | | | |
| 32 | 3 | Tharsis Street | | | | | | |
| 31 | 4 | 3 | Castle Street at Parliamentary Rd | | | | | |
| 30 | 6 | 4 | 3 | Cathedral Street or Duke Street | | | | |
| 29 | 6 | 6 | 4 | 3 | Glasgow Cross | | | |
| 28 | 9 | 6 | 6 | 4 | 3 | Rutherglen Road | | |
| 27 | 9 | 9 | 6 | 6 | 4 | 3 | Aikenhead Road at Cathcart Road | |
| 26 | 10 | 9 | 9 | 6 | 6 | 4 | 3 | Polmadie (Brereton Street at Calder Street) |
| 25 | 10 | 10 | 9 | 9 | 6 | 6 | 4 | 3 | Hampden Garage |

Fare Chart (July 1964)

28. BUT TB26 waits at the Polmadie Street stop in Aikenhead Road on Service 103 to Hampden Park in 1958. The right hand turn into the Polmadie terminal loop is just out of view on the left, and the return leg to regain Aikenhead Road at the junction with Calder Street can just be seen in the background. The Service 103 extension further along Aikenhead Road, and then King's Park Avenue to Hampden Park, was introduced in August 1950, and withdrawn in May 1959. Return journeys from Hampden Park to Riddrie displayed Service 102. (R F Mack/S Fozard copyright)

29. The Polmadie terminus of Service 102 has been reached by BUT TB1, and is seen turning out of Aikenhead Road into Bennan Square in September 1962, which was a short length of road that led into the actual square. Before the square is reached, TB1 will turn right into Brereton Street where the layover stand is located. The box van to the rear is an Albion owned by Crimpy Potato Crisps of Airdrie, and the building to the rear has been replaced by the single storey International Bar. (C Routh)

30.   At the terminal stand in Brereton Street, Daimler TD20 waits to make a return trip to Riddrie along the remainder of the loop leading into Calder Street, and then Aikenhead Road.  The majority of Glasgow's trolleybus terminal points were of a "round the houses" configuration.  (P Mitchell)

## 102   ROYSTON ROAD to POLMADIE

| Week-days a.m. | p.m. | p.m. | Sats. a.m. | p.m. | Suns. a.m. | p.m. |
|---|---|---|---|---|---|---|
| 7 11 | 12 9 | 11 54 | 7 52 | — | 8 33 | 2 55 |
| 6 ms | 12 ms | — | 7 11 | 8 2 | 8 55 | Same |
| 7 59 | 2 33 | | 15 ms | 15 ms | 20 ms | each |
| 8 5s | 15 ms | | 9 56 | 9 47 | p.m. | hour |
| 8 11 | 4 33 | | 10 10 | 10 1 | 12 35 | till |
| 6 ms | 47 | | 10 ms | 12 ms | 15 ms | 5 40 |
| 8 53 | 4 53 | | 11 40 | 11 1 | 1 50 | 15 ms |
| 9 0 | 6 ms | | 47 | 12 | 2 2 | 11 10 |
| 8 | 6 5 | | 55 | 24 | 10 | 24 |
| 9 15 | 17 | | p.m. | 36 | 17 | 39 |
| 15 ms | 25 | | 12 3 | 48 | 25 | 54 |
| 11 45 | 39 | | 8 ms | 56 | 32 | |
| 57 | 54 | | 6 27 | | 40 | |
| | 7 9 | | 6 40 | | 47 | |
| | 15 ms | | 12 ms | | | |

## 102   POLMADIE to ROYSTON ROAD

| Week-days a.m. | p.m. | Sats. a.m. | p.m. | Suns. a.m. | p.m. | p.m. |
|---|---|---|---|---|---|---|
| 6 48 | 12 ms | 7 29 | — | 1 48 | 5 18 | |
| 6 ms | 2 10 | 6 48 | 7 40 | 7 0c | 55 | 5 32 |
| 8 30 | 2 20 | 7 4 | 15 ms | 30c | 2 3 | 15 ms |
| 37 | 15 ms | 15 ms | 9 25 | 8 12 | 10 | 11 32 |
| 45 | 4 20 | 9 34 | 39 | 34 | 18 | |
| 52 | 4 29 | 9 48 | 9 50 | 54 | 25 | |
| 9 0 | 6 ms | 10 ms | 12 ms | 9 14 | 33 | |
| 15 ms | 5 41 | 11 18 | 11 26 | 9 18 | 40 | |
| 11 45 | 52 | 11 24 | 34 | 20 ms | 48 | |
| 58 | 6 0 | 8 ms | — | p.m. | 55 | |
| p.m. | 16 | p.m. | | 12 58 | Same | |
| 12 10 | 6 32 | 6 4 | | 1 13 | each | |
| | 15 ms | 6 17 | | 28 | hour | |
| | 11 32 | 12 ms | | 38 | till | |

| s To Shawfield | c To Cathedral St. |
|---|---|

| Royston Rd. to Castle St. | .. | 5 mins. |
|---|---|---|
| Castle St. to Glasgow Cross | .. | 7 „ |
| Glasgow Cross to Polmadie | .. | 9 „ |

Timetable (November 1962)

31.   Service 103 continued along Aikenhead Road, before turning into King's Park Avenue to reach the Hampden Park terminus.  The terminal loop was along Carmunnock and Ballogie Roads; Sunbeam TG7 is at the terminal stand in the latter location ready to return to Riddrie displaying Service 102.  On leaving, it will turn left into King's Park Road, and then immediately return along King's Park Avenue.  The section insulator to the rear is again identified by the white band on the traction standard. (P Mitchell)

# QUEEN'S CROSS TO COWCADDENS STREET
# (NOW ROAD) (SERVICE 105)

32. At the northern Queen's Cross terminus of Service 105, BUT TB124 turns out of Garscube Road into Springbank Street in May 1967, as it enters the first section of the terminal loop; the destination blind has already been set for a short working return journey back to Mount Florida. The corner shop is now occupied by Co-op Funeralcare, and modern apartments have replaced the tenements in the background adjacent to a widened road.  (D Smithies)

**105 QUEEN'S CROSS to BALLOGIE RD. or MUIREND or CLARKSTON**

| Week-days a.m. | a.m. | p.m. | p.m. | a.m. | p.m. | p.m. |
|---|---|---|---|---|---|---|
| 5 40 | 9 6§ | 2 2§ | 6 49* | 7 14 | 5 24* | 8 30 |
| 54 | 10 | 5* | 54 | 19* | 27 | 12 ms |
| 6 14 | 15* | 9 | 59* | 24 | 30* | p.m. |
| 34 | 9 20 | 2 13* | 7 4 | 29* | 33 | 1 18 |
| 54 | 5 ms | 4 ms | 7 9* | 34 | 36* | 31 |
| 7 4 | Alt. | Alt. | 5 ms | 38* | 39 | 43 |
| 10 | Ball. | Ball. | Alt. | 42 | 42* | 55 |
| 18† | Clark | Clark | Ball. | 46* | 5 45 | 2 0† |
| 21 | 11 35* | 3 25* | Clark | 49 | 3 ms | 5 |
| 24† | 40 | 29 | 10 19* | 53* | Alt. | 10† |
| 27 | 44† | 33† | 24 | 7 57 | Ball. | 15 |
| 30† | 50† | 37 | 29† | 4 ms | Clark | 20† |
| 33 | 56† | 41† | 34 | Alt. | 10 36* | 25 |
| 39 | 59 | 3 45 | 40† | Ball. | 39 | 30† |
| 7 42† | p.m. | 4 ms | 46 | Clark | 44† | 35 |
| 3 ms | 12 5 | 4 29 | 50* | 11 29* | 45 | 40† |
| Alt. | 11 | 35 | 54† | 33 | 48† | 45 |
| Clark | 14† | 38 | 59* | 39† | 51* | 50† |
| Muir | 20† | 41 | 11 4† | 42 | 54† | 55 |
| 8 15 | 23 | 47 | 9* | 45† | 57* | 3 0† |
| 21 | 3 ms | 50 | 14† | 51† | 11 0† | Same |
| 24† | Alt. | 53 | 19* | 54 | 3* | each |
| 27† | Muir | 4 59 | 24† | 57† | 6† | hour |
| 30* | Clark | 3 ms | 31† | p.m. | 9* | till |
| 33 | 1 23 | 5 59 | 41§ | 12 3† | 12† | 10 40† |
| 36† | 26† | 6 2* | 51§ | 12 6 | 15* | 46 |
| 39* | 29 | 5 | 12 6§ | 3 ms | 18† | 50† |
| 42 | 32§ | 8* | Sats. | Alt. | 24† | 55* |
| 45* | 35 | 11 | a.m. | Muir | 30† | 11 0† |
| 48§ | 38§ | 14§ | 5 40 | Clark | 36§ | 5* |
| 51 | 41* | 17 | 54 | 5 3† | 42§ | 10† |
| 54* | 44 | 20§ | 6 14 | 6 | 48§ | 15* |
| 57§ | 47§ | 26 | 30 | 9* | 54§ | 20† |
| 9 0 | 50* | 29§ | 37 | 12 | 12 6§ | 25* |
| 3* | 53 | 34 | 54 | 15 | Suns. | 31† |
|  | 56* | 39† | 7 4 | 18* | a.m. | 40§ |
|  | 59 | 44 | 10* | 21 | 8 15 | 50§ |
|  |  |  |  |  |  | 12 6§ |

Unmarked to Clarkston    * To Ballogie Rd.
§ To Hampden Gar. via Polmadie   † To M'rend

Timetable (November 1962)

33.   BUT TB42 leaves Firhill Road, the second leg of the terminal loop, and enters Northpark Street to reach the terminal stand; in the distance another vehicle exits Springbank Street.  Firhill Stadium, the home of Partick Thistle Football Club, dominates the background; in the past the facility has also been used by Clyde and Hamilton Academicals football clubs on a temporary basis. It also housed Glasgow Warriors Rugby Club for a period, and rugby league has also been played there on occasions. (P Mitchell)

34.   BUT TB21 waits at the terminal stand in Northpark Street before departing across the city to Clarkston. Two and three storey housing has replaced the buildings depicted, although further along the street towards Maryhill Road the old four storey buildings remain.
(Travel Lens Photographic)

35.    Having travelled around the terminal loop, BUT TB1 turns out of Northpark Street into Maryhill Road, and will immediately join Garscube Road on a short working to Mount Florida in April 1960.  The ground floor of the four storey building is now occupied by another funeral directors, but the buildings beyond have disappeared.  Note the tram track and overhead wiring are still in place along Maryhill Road for Services 18/18A/23 and 29, plus the Morris van in the foreground.  (R F Mack/NTA)

---

**Trolleybus Service No. 105**

**QUEEN'S CROSS and CLARKSTON**

**No Weekly Tickets**

*Stage No.*

| 33 | Queen's Cross (Northpark Street) |
|----|----|
| 32 | 3   Cedar Street |
| 31 | 4   3   New City Road, 1 |
| 30 | 6   4   3   West Nile Street, 44 |
| 29 | 6   6   4   3   Trongate |
| 28 | 9   6   6   4   3   Cleland Street |
| 27 | 9   9   6   6   4   3   Aikenhead Road |
| 26 | 10   9   9   6   6   4   3   Dixon Avenue |
| 25 | 10   10   9   9   6   6   4   3   Mount Florida |
| 24 | 1s   10   10   9   9   6   6   4   3   Cathcart Railway Bridge |
| 23 | 1s   1s   10   10   9   9   6   6   4   3   Cathcart Cemetery Gate |
| 22 | 1s   1s   1s   10   10   9   9   6   6   4   3   Netherlee |
| 21 | 1s   1s   1s   1s   10   10   9   9   6   6   4   3   Stamperland Gardens |
| 20 | 1s   1s   1s   1s   1s   10   10   9   9   6   6   4   3   Clarkston (Mearns Rd) |
| 24 | 1s   10   10   9   9   6   6   4   3   Ballogie Road |
| 23 | 1s   1s   10   10   9   9   6   6   4   3   Hampden Garage |
| 22 | 1s   1s   1s   10   10   9   9   6   6   4   3   Muirend Terminus |

Fare Chart (July 1964)

36.   BUT TB113 moves down Garscube Road on its way to Clarkston, followed closely behind by a Leyland PD3 motorbus L353 (SGD 355), badged Albion Titan, and destined for Shettleston. The front of an Austin K8 van can be seen in Grovepark Street next to the four storey building, which has large windows at roof level. In 1939 at least the ground floor was used by a valet service company, whose sign board can be seen above the Austin van; in 1950, and up to 1960, the Sterling Spring Coil Company occupied the premises.  Note the barber's pole on the left; this scene is unrecognisable today. (P Mitchell)

37.   At the Round Toll BUT TB108, destined for Clarkston, crosses the junction with Possil Road on the right, and St George's Road to the left.  Tram track and overhead wiring for tram Service 16 are in evidence between the two roads, with Bedford and Fordson vans in the background.  Note the pawnbroker's sign, and that the shop on the corner has suffered a broken window; the owner has used it to his advantage by displaying a notice which says "Another Smash Hit".  This scene is also unrecognisable today.  (R F Mack/NTA)

38. At the southern end of Garscube Road BUT TB124 is about to pass under a section insulator, and join Cowcaddens Street on a short working to Mount Florida. To the right of this view was the Phoenix Recreation Ground, but most of this scene has disappeared under the M8 Motorway; the only point of reference today is Corn Street a little further back on the right. (R F Mack/S Fozard copyright)

## COWCADDENS STREET (NOW ROAD) TO GEORGE SQUARE (SERVICES 105/107)

39. We now reach the northern terminus of Service 107 (Maitland Street), which joined with the 105 at Cowcaddens Street, to share wiring south to the junction of Gorbals Street and Cathcart Road, after which they parted company until rejoining at Homlea Road. BUT TB111 leaves Maitland Street, the last leg of the terminal loop, having traversed Port Dundas Road and Milton Street, and enters Cowcaddens Street en route to Muirend. This junction is now closed off, and a multi storey block of flats occupies the land to the rear of TB111. Note the tram track leading into Hope Street. (R F Mack/NTA)

**107  MUIREND to MAITLAND ST.**

| Week-days a.m. | p.m. | Sats. a.m. | p.m. | p.m. | Suns. a.m. |
|---|---|---|---|---|---|
| 11 36 | 6 26* | 5 44* | 9 41 | a.m. |  |
| 52 | 39 | 56 | 57 | 9 5 |  |
| .7 0 | 46* | 15 ms | 6 13 | 10 13 | 20 ms |
| p.m. | 7 5 | 8 30 | 29 | 29 | p.m. |
| 12 8 | 11* | 10 ms | 32* | 45 | 11 5 |
| 12 20 | 7 25 | p.m. | 45 | 11 5 | 26* |
| 10 ms | 4 30 | 1 10 | 7 1 | 16* | 47* |
| 7 48 | 4 38 | 11 5 | 17 | 32* | 12 8* |
| 6 ms | 11 5 | 22 | 33 | 49* |  |
| 9 0 | 6 ms | 34 | 49 | 12 9* |  |
| 10 ms | 5 38 | 47 | 8 5 |  |  |
| 10 0 | 48 | 49* | 21 |  |  |
| 16 | 49* | 59 | 37 |  |  |
| 32 | 50* | 2 11 | 53 |  |  |
| 48 | 58 | 37 | 9 9 |  |  |
| 11 4 | 6 2* | 53 | 25 |  |  |
| 20 | 19 | 5 23 |  |  |  |
|  | 20* | 39 |  |  |  |

\* To Hampden Garage via Ballogie Road.

**107  MAITLAND ST. to MUIREND**

| Week-days a.m. | a.m. | p.m. | a.m. | p.m. | p.m. |
|---|---|---|---|---|---|
| 8 58 | 10 49 | 6 20 | 15 ms | 7 17 | 10 45 |
| 9 4§ | 11 5 | 30 | 8 56 | 33 | 11 1 |
| 7 23 | 8 | 40 | 9 7 | 49 | 18 |
| 34 | 14§ | 6 50 | 10 ms | 8 5 | 38 |
| 46 | 19 | 20 ms | p.m. | 21 | Suns. |
| 58 | 29 | 10 ms | 1 37 | 37 | a.m. |
| 8 10 | 31§ | p.m. | 48 | 53 | 9 35 |
| 22 | 45 | 38 | 2 1 | 9 9 | 20 m |
| 28 | 51§ | 58 | 11 18 | 25 | p.m. |
| 34 | 10 1 | 4 6 | 38 | 41 | 10 35 |
| 38§ | 17 | 6 ms | 6 13 | 57 | 56 |
| 46 | 21§ | 6 0 | Sats. | 10 13 | 11 17 |
| 50§ | 33 | 4§ | a.m. | 29 | 38 |
|  |  | 10 | 7 41 | 7 1 |  |

| Muirend to Battlefield | .. | .. | 9 mins. |
|---|---|---|---|
| Battlefield to Eglinton Toll | .. | .. | 6 ,, |
| Eglinton Toll to Trongate | .. | .. | 7 ,, |
| Trongate to Maitland St. | .. | .. | 8 ,, |

§To Hampden Garage via Polmadie.

40. This scene is unrecognisable today as BUT TB113 travels along Cowcaddens Street, past the end of Milton Street in August 1961, on a short working of Service 105 to Mount Florida. Milton Street no longer joins Cowcaddens Street, but the location is roughly opposite the current junction with Cambridge Street on the opposite side of the road. In the background is Cunarder tram 1378 on Service 29 to Tollcross. (C Routh)

Timetable (November 1962)

41.  A virtually empty BUT TB72 is about to leave Cowcaddens Street and enter West Nile Street on Service 107 to Muirend.  The overhead wiring leaving the picture top right led into Port Dundas Road, which was the first leg of the Maitland Street terminal loop.  Behind TB72 is the erstwhile Buchanan Street Station Hotel, serving the named station which was opposite, with the less imposing Caledonian Hotel next door.  (S Lockwood collection)

42.  With the rear of the Empire Theatre on the left, BUT TB112 has travelled further south down West Nile Street on Service 107 to Muirend.  The main entrance to the theatre was around the corner in Sauchiehall Street, and entertained a wide variety of acts, with the last performance occuring on 31st March 1963.  The site is now occupied by the Empire House office/retail complex.  The car on the right is a Ford Consul II.  (P Mitchell)

43.   BUT TB14, with full destination display, passes the end of West Regent Street as it travels down West Nile Street on Service 105 as far as Muirend; there are three other trolleybuses in the distance.  The building on the corner has been replaced by a modern glass fronted office block. Other vehicles in view include a high roof Austin A40 van, the rear of a Ford Prefect, and a Hillman Husky on the left. (P Mitchell)

44.   Sunbeam TG2 has turned short at George Square, on a northern journey of Service 105.  This vehicle is one of five with distinctive bodywork by Alexander; the company only built one other trolleybus body, which was for an experimental South Yorkshire PTE vehicle.  TG2 is just about to leave Hanover Street, the last leg of the terminal loop having entered from Ingram Street, and is destined for Mount Florida; this was the city terminus of Night Service 5.  The news vendor appears to be enjoying brisk business.  (R F Mack/NTA)

45. Two BUTs carrying differing liveries, with TB78 leading, painted in a short lived experimental reversed livery of yellow upper/green lower, and TB119 to the rear. They are passing along the south side of George Square, both on Service 105, and are destined for Mount Florida and Clarkston respectively. The overhead wiring coming in from the left is the exit from Hanover Street, last leg of the terminal loop referred to in the previous picture. On the left is a Morris Minor, and opposite a Vauxhall Victor. (S J Brown)

# GEORGE SQUARE TO CATHCART ROAD
## (SERVICES 5/105/107)

46.  Having left George Square, with the original General Post Office building as a backdrop, BUT TB113 has just turned out of South Frederick Street into Ingram Street on Service 105 to Clarkston, and will almost immediately turn right into Glassford Street.  A Ford Consul travels in the opposite direction.  (P Mitchell)

47.  A Volkswagen Beetle passes BUT TB109 travelling north along Glassford Street on Service 105 to Queen's Cross.  In the distance is the railway overbridge which carried lines into the LMSR St Enoch Station, now the site of retail outlets in the St Enoch Centre.  Beyond the Volkswagen is a Morris Commercial LC5 lorry.  (P Mitchell)

48.  BUT TB44 on Service 107 has left Glassford Street, and having travelled along Stockwell Street,  now crosses Victoria Bridge over the River Clyde; it will shortly enter Gorbals Street and onwards to Muirend.  The bridge is devoid of traffic, other than the following unidentified Corporation Daimler motorbus.  (Author's collection)

49.   In this busier scene on the bridge, Daimler TD12 travels in the opposite direction on Service 105 to Queen's Cross with a good complement of passengers.  TD12 has travelled along Gorbals Street from its junction with Cathcart Road to reach the bridge approach.  The buildings to the rear of the Leyland lorry have made way for the Glasgow Sheriff, Justice of the Peace and Stipendiary Magistrate Courts. (S Lockwood collection)

# CATHCART ROAD TO HOLMLEA ROAD VIA CATHCART ROAD (SERVICES 104/105)

50.    Leaving Services 5 and 107 to follow their separate route to Holmlea Road, BUT TB110 is seen in Cathcart Road on Service 105 to Mount Florida.  Govanhill Parish Church, which has since been demolished, is on the left, with a Ford Classic waiting to leave Allison Street served by Service 108.  (Also see Picture 95).  TB110 has just passed under an electrical feeder supply, and on the left hand traction standard a direction indicator can be seen, which showed drivers the setting of the automatic overhead junction turnout leading into Allison Street.  These driver controlled automatic turnout junctions were eventually discontinued, leaving conductors, or more normally conductresses, to alight and change direction using short hooked poles carried on each vehicle, to reach the higher mounted pull handle, with consequent interruptions to traffic flows. (P Mitchell)

51.   Further along Cathcart Road, between Cumming Drive and Stanmore Road, BUT TB102 is on a short working of Service 105 to Mount Florida, and will shortly turn left into King's Park Road to reach the terminal point.  This stretch of overhead wiring was shared with Service 108 from King's Park Road as far as Allison Street.  A BRS lorry follows close behind.  (P Mitchell)

52.   At the junction of Cathcart Road and King's Park Road, BUT TB72 takes the former to Muirend; the vehicle in the previous picture would take the road on the right.  The Cathkinview Place tower block, and the tenements on the right remain; the car in the foreground is a Ford Anglia Estate. (R F Mack/NTA)

53.   Sunbeam TG11 has nearly completed its journey south on a short working of Service 105 to Mount Florida, and is about to leave King's Park Road and enter the short link into Carmunnock Road, which is the first leg of the terminal loop; the overhead turnout junction can be seen at the top of the picture.  The destination display has already been changed for the return to Queen's Cross. On the left is a Morris Minor Traveller, and a Singer Gazelle.  (P Mitchell)

# CATHCART ROAD TO HOLMLEA ROAD VIA VICTORIA ROAD (SERVICES 5/107)

*We return now to Gorbals Street, where Services 5/107 leave the 104/105 to make their separate way to Holmlea Road, and onwards towards Muirend. On leaving Gorbals Street, vehicles travelled along Pollokshaws Road into Victoria Road.*

54.  Towards the southern end of Victoria Road BUT TB39 will shortly leave the stop, and travel a short distance before turning into Queen's Drive in August 1957. Tram track and overhead wiring are still in evidence for Service 5, which was withdrawn three and a half months later, the trolleybus service having commenced just under a month earlier. Tram infrastructure continued in use until the replacement of tram Service 24 by bus Service 44 in March 1958. A short distance behind is Queen's Park Station, and in the far distance is Allison Street where trolleybus Service 108 crossed Victoria Road. (D Smithies)

55.  A little further on from the previous picture BUT TB46 begins the turn out of Victoria Road into Queen's Drive.  There has been little change to this scene over the years as a Morris Minor overtakes, and a Wolseley car brings up the rear.  (P Mitchell)

56.  BUT TB74, in spray painted livery, is about to leave Queen's Drive and enter Langside Road en route to Muirend in May 1967.  On the left is the boundary fence of the extensive Queen's Park, one of the many parks created in the Victorian era to provide open spaces for the ever increasing population.  It was dedicated to Mary Queen of Scots who lost the Battle of Langside nearby. (D Smithies)

57.   This August 1957 view depicts BUT TB35 in Holmlea Road passing Coronation car 1183, with a second car 1174 further back opposite the side entrance to Langside tram depot. The scene illustrates the tram terminus for truncated Services 5/5A, which had previously run to Clarkston. At the time the photograph was taken the depot was undergoing conversion to a motorbus garage. Originally opened in 1901, it closed in 1984, and was subsequently demolished to make way for domestic housing. (D Smithies)

58.   BUT TB105 passes the end of Ruel Street in Holmlea Road, and is about to re-join the shared overhead wiring with Services 104 and 105, the latter entering from Cathcart Road on the right. All four services will now travel along Clarkston Road towards Muirend.   (P Mitchell)

# HOLMLEA ROAD TO MUIREND
## (SERVICES 5/104/105/107)

59. BUT TB4 has arrived at Muirend on Service 105, and has encountered a Bedford tower wagon, with linesmen working on the overhead turnout junction from Clarkston Road into Muirend Road. Consequently TB4 has booms lowered to pass the obstruction, and moves into the latter under battery power in September 1962, with the blind set for the return journey to Queen's Cross. The buildings are unchanged, other than the retailers occupying them. (C Routh)

60. On a return journey north to Maitland Street on Service 107, BUT TB111 has just left the Muirend turning circle, one of only three on the system (two specially constructed). Adjacent properties are unchanged, but there is now a pedestrian crossing controlled by traffic lights immediately in front of the vehicle's position. (P Mitchell)

61.   BUT TB68 waits in the Muirend turning circle, which was used by trolleybus Services 104/105/107, before returning to Cathedral Street on the former, although the destination indicator has still to be changed.  The circle was used by motorbus Service 67 after trolleybus Service 107 ceased.  (P Mitchell)

**Trolleybus Service No. 107**

**MUIREND and MAITLAND STREET**

**No Weekly Tickets**

| Stage No. | | | | | | | | | |
|---|---|---|---|---|---|---|---|---|---|
| 22 | Muirend (Muirend Road at Harelaw Avenue) |
| 23 | 3 Cathcart Cemetery Gate |
| 24 | 4 | 3 | Cathcart Railway Bridge |
| 25 | 6 | 4 | 3 | Battlefield |
| 26 | 6 | 6 | 4 | 3 | Queen's Park (Victoria Road Gate) |
| 27 | 9 | 6 | 6 | 4 | 3 | Eglinton Toll |
| 28 | 9 | 9 | 6 | 6 | 4 | 3 | Cleland Street |
| 29 | 10 | 9 | 9 | 6 | 6 | 4 | 3 | Trongate |
| 30 | 10 | 10 | 9 | 9 | 6 | 6 | 4 | 3 | West Nile Street, 44 |
| 31 | 1s | 10 | 10 | 9 | 9 | 6 | 6 | 4 | 3 Maitland Street |

Fare Chart (July 1964)

62. On a rather murky day the original "standee" BUT TBS1 (originally TB35) is about to leave the Muirend terminus, also on Service 104 to Cathedral Street. It is in its original design format and livery, including a full destination display. Note the use of the curved twin line hangers to create the overhead wiring circle.
(H Luff/Online Transport Archive)

Timetable (November 1962)

## 105   MUIREND to QUEEN'S CROSS

| Week-days a.m. | p.m. | p.m. | Sats. a.m. | p.m. | Suns. a.m. | p.m. |
|---|---|---|---|---|---|---|
|       | 12 26 | 11 40H | | 11 32H | | 11 56H |
| a.m.  | 12 29 | 50H | 5 2 | 38H | 7 38 | 12 7H |
| 5 2   | 6 ms | 12 0H | ---- | 44H | 8 5 | |
| 7 5   | 1 29 | 7H | p.m. | 50H | 32 | |
| 32    | 35† | | 12 18 | 56H | | |
| 7 50  | 41 | | 27 | 12 2H | p.m. | |
| 6 ms  | 47† | | 12 30 | 8H | 2 9 | |
| 8 26  | 53 | | 6 ms | | 10 ms | |
| 32*   | 59† | | 1 30 | | 10 49 | |
| 38†   | 2 5 | | 1 37 | | 56H | |
| 44    | 4 15 | | 6 ms | | 11 6H | |
| 50†   | 23 | | 5 43 | | 16H | |
| 9 2†  | 5 1 | | | | 26H | |
| 10    | 11 16H | | 11 22H | | 36H | |
| 20    | 30H | | 26H | | 46H | |

* To Maitland St.     † To George Square
H To Hampden Gar. via Ballogie Rd.
ms Minute Service

## 105   BALLOGIE RD. to QUEEN'S CROSS

| Week-days a.m. | p.m. | p.m. | Sats. a.m. | p.m. | Suns. a.m. |
|---|---|---|---|---|---|
|       | 7 51 | 2 30† | | 12 19 | |
| a.m.  | ---- | 2 37 | 4 56† | 28 | 7 56 |
| 4 56† | 9 37 | 8 ms | 5 20† | ---- | 8 50 |
| 5 20† | 10 ms | 4 13 | 6 33 | 5 56 | |
| 6 33  | 11 37 | 32 | 48 | 6 2 | p.m. |
| 45    | 48 | 38 | 7 5 | 6 14 | 1 32 |
| 51    | 57 | 5 20 | 8 ms | 6 ms | 41 |
| 7 0   | p.m. | | 11 37 | 10 44 | 46 |
| 6     | 12 9 | 7 19 | 46 | | 56 |
| 15    | 27 | 10 ms | 55 | | 2 5 |
| 21    | | 10 49 | p.m. | | |
| 27    | 2 18† | | 12 1 | | |
| 33    | 24 | | 10 | | |

† To George Square     ms Minute Service

# MUIREND TO CLARKSTON
## (SERVICES 5/105)

63. Sunbeam TG1 is seen travelling south along Clarkston Road towards the Clarkston terminus; the destination blind has already been changed for the return to Queen's Cross. It is passing the privately run Williamwood Golf Course, which is on the left. The road is deserted, other than the parked Mini. (P Mitchell)

64. At the end of the journey south, BUT TB115 arrives at Clarkston in September 1962, and has entered the start of the terminal loop in Busby Road; again the destination blind has been changed for the return to journey. It will next enter Mearns Road, where the layover will be taken, before travelling along Benview Road to re-join Clarkston Road, where the Western SMT motor bus is about to cross the railway bridge. (C Routh)

65. At the layover point in Mearns Road, Daimler TD3 waits to return to Queen's Cross, with an Alexander bodied Sunbeam behind: note the contrasting liveries. A Triumph Herald saloon completes the picture. (P Mitchell)

**105  CLARKSTON to QUEEN'S CROSS**

| Week-days a.m. | p.m. | p.m. | p.m. | Sats. a.m. | p.m. | Suns. a.m. |
|---|---|---|---|---|---|---|
| 12 18 | 6 ms | 5 35 | 6 34H | 5 11 | 6 ms | 6 26† |
| 12 27 | 2 21 | 38H | 6 37 | 31 | 1 28 | 7 7† |
| 5 11 | 2 29 | 41 | 7 2 | 54 | 1 35 | 8 14 |
| 31 | 8 ms | 45 | 10 42 | 6 11 | 6 ms | 49 |
| 51 | 4 13 | 47H | 49 | 27 | 5 53 | 9 1 |
| 6 11 | 23 | 49 | 59 | 45 | 56 | 12 ms |
| 27 | 29 | 52H | 11 9 | 57 | 59 | p.m. |
| 45 | 35 | 55 | 19 | 7 5 | 6 5 | 1 25 |
| 57 | 38 | 58H | 28H | 8 ms | 6 ms | 39 |
| 7 6 | 41 | 6 1 | | 11 21 | 11 11 | 1 48 |
| 6 ms | 47 | 4H | | 31 | 19 | 10 ms |
| 9 0 | 50 | 7 | | 37 | 22H | 11 8 |
| 10 ms | 53 | 12 | | 46 | 28H | 19 |
| 11 30 | 59 | 14H | | 55 | | 28H |
| 39 | 5 2 | 17 | | p.m. | | |
| 51 | 5 | 19H | | 12 1 | | |
| p.m. | 5 11 | 22 | | 10 | | |
| 12 0 | 3 ms | 27 | | 19 | | |
| 6 | | 29H | | 28 | | |
| 12 | | 32 | | | | |

H To Hampden Gar. via Ballogie Rd
† To George Square    *ms* Minute Service

| | | |
|---|---|---|
| Clarkston to Mt. Florida | .. | 14 mins. |
| Muirend to Mt. Florida .. | .. | 9 ,, |
| Ballogie Rd. to Mt. Florida | .. | 2 ,, |
| Mt. Florida to Trongate | .. | 12 ,, |
| Trongate to Normal School | | 9 ,, |
| Normal School to Queen's X | .. | 7 ,, |

Timetable (November 1962)

66.  Sunbeam TG7 takes the sharp turn out of Mearns Road into Benview Road to enter the last leg of the terminal loop.  Note the use of curved twin line hangers again to create the wiring radius. (P Mitchell)

67.  The same vehicle as in Picture 65, with the photograph probably taken on the same day judging by the destination blind position, travels along Benview Road as it passes Sunnyside Drive.  It will shortly re-join Clarkston Road to begin the journey back to Queen's Cross.  A Morris Minor and a Ford Prefect follow behind.  (P Mitchell)

↗     68.  The Millerston terminus was provided with one of the two specially constructed turning facilities, the other being at Muirend; the third turning circle was round a traffic island at Shieldhall. Other than the above, "round the houses" terminal loops were the order of the day.  BUT TB93 waits in the circle to return south, which was located in Station Road adjacent to Craigbarnet Crescent, accompanied by Leyland PD2 motorbus L154 on a short working of Service 38 to Argyle Street. (V Nutton/Travel Lens Photographic)

# MILLERSTON TO BRIDGETON CROSS
## (SERVICE 106)

## 106 RIDDRIE (TEITH ST.) to BELLAHOUSTON

| Week-days a.m. | p.m. | p.m. | a.m. | p.m. | p.m. | p.m. |
|---|---|---|---|---|---|---|
| | 3 45 | 11 28† | 9 6 | 9 9 | 12 29 | 11 36† |
| 5 11 | 49 | 33† | 9 10 | 9 15 | 35 | 41† |
| 30 | 55 | 36† | 5 ms | 5 ms | 47 | 48† |
| 46 | 58 | 41† | 11 25 | 10 45 | 59 | 58† |
| 52* | 4 4 | 48† | 28 | 10 51 | 1 11 | 12 8† |
| 6 5 | 10 | 58† | 34 | 5 ms | 1 23 | |
| 6 20 | 13 | 12 8† | 40 | 11 26 | 6 ms | |
| 8 ms | 19 | | 43 | 33† | 1 53 | |
| 7 0 | 25 | Sats. | 46 | 36† | 58 | |
| 4 ms | 28 | a.m. | 52 | 41† | 2 4 | |
| 8 20 | 31 | 5 11 | 58 | 48† | 6 ms | |
| 24† | 4 37 | 30 | p.m. | 58† | 4 28 | |
| 28 | 3 ms | 52* | 12 1 | 12 8† | 5 ms | |
| 32 | 5 40 | 20 | 5 25 | | 5 58 | |
| 36† | 43† | 28 | 28† | | 6 4 | |
| 40 | 46 | 40 | 31 | Suns. | 10 | |
| 44† | 49 | 52 | 34† | a.m. | 12† | |
| 48 | 52 | 55† | 37 | 6 35 | 16 | |
| 52† | 55† | 7 0 | 40 | 48 | 22 | |
| 56 | 58 | 8 | 43† | 7 10 | 28 | |
| 9 0† | 6 1 | 12 | 46 | 40 | 31† | |
| 4 | 4 | 20 | 49† | 8 13* | 6 34 | |
| 11 | 7† | 24 | 52 | 8 46 | 6 ms | |
| 9 19 | 6 10 | 7 32 | 55† | 9 19 | 8 58 | |
| 7½ ms | 6 ms | 4 ms | 58 | 10 31 | 5 ms | |
| 10 49 | 9 16 | 8 24 | 6 3 | 42† | 10 53 | |
| 57 | 21 | 28† | | 46 | 56 | |
| 11 5 | 26 | 32 | 5† | | |
| 12 | 5 ms | 36 | 8 | 11 1 | 11 1 | |
| 20 | 9 36 | 40 | 10† | 16 | 6 | |
| 27 | 11 1 | 44 | 6 13 | 31 | 11 | |
| 35 | 8 | 48† | 5 ms | 48 | 16 | |
| 11 45 | 12† | 52 | 7 28 | p.m. | 24 | |
| 5 ms | 16 | 56 | 7 34 | 12 1 | 26† | |
| | 23 | 9 0 | 5 ms | 16 | 33† | |

\* To Shieldhall      † To Govan Garage
ms Minute Service

Timetable (November 1962)

---

## Trolleybus Service No. 106
## MILLERSTON and BELLAHOUSTON
### No Weekly Tickets

| Stage No. | | | | | | | | | | | | | | |
|---|---|---|---|---|---|---|---|---|---|---|---|---|---|---|
| 20 | | | | | | | | | | | | | | Millerston (Station Road) |
| 21 | 3 | | | | | | | | | | | | | Hogganfield |
| 22 | 4 | 3 | | | | | | | | | | | | Riddrie (Tay Crescent) |
| 23 | 6 | 4 | 3 | | | | | | | | | | | Gough Street |
| 24 | 6 | 6 | 4 | 3 | | | | | | | | | | Aitken Street |
| 25 | 9 | 6 | 6 | 4 | 3 | | | | | | | | | Millerston Street |
| 26 | 9 | 9 | 6 | 6 | 4 | 3 | | | | | | | | Bellgrove Station |
| 27 | 10 | 9 | 9 | 6 | 6 | 4 | 3 | | | | | | | Bridgeton Cross |
| 28 | 10 | 10 | 9 | 9 | 6 | 6 | 4 | 3 | | | | | | McNeil Street |
| 29 | 1s | 10 | 10 | 9 | 9 | 6 | 6 | 4 | 3 | | | | | Crown Street |
| 30 | 1s | 1s | 10 | 10 | 9 | 9 | 6 | 6 | 4 | 3 | | | | West Street |
| 31 | 1s | 1s | 1s | 10 | 10 | 9 | 9 | 6 | 6 | 4 | 3 | | | Paisley Road Toll |
| 32 | 1s | 1s | 1s | 1s | 10 | 10 | 9 | 9 | 6 | 6 | 4 | 3 | | Lorne School |
| 33 | 1s | 1s | 1s | 1s | 1s | 10 | 10 | 9 | 9 | 6 | 6 | 4 | 3 | Summertown Road |
| 34 | 1s | 1s | 1s | 1s | 1s | 1s | 10 | 10 | 9 | 9 | 6 | 6 | 4 | 3 | Govan Cross |
| 35 | 1s | 1s | 1s | 1s | 1s | 1s | 1s | 10 | 10 | 9 | 9 | 6 | 6 | 4 | 3 | Luss Road |
| 36 | 1s | 1s | 1s | 1s | 1s | 1s | 1s | 1s | 10 | 10 | 9 | 9 | 6 | 6 | 4 | 3 | Bellahouston (Minto Street) |
| 35 | 1s | 1s | 1s | 1s | 1s | 1s | 1s | 10 | 10 | 9 | 9 | 6 | 6 | 4 | 3 | Govan Road at Moss Rd |
| 36 | 1s | 1s | 1s | 1s | 1s | 1s | 1s | 1s | 10 | 10 | 9 | 9 | 6 | 6 | 4 | 3 | Bogmoor Road |
| 37 | 1s | 1s | 1s | 1s | 1s | 1s | 1s | 1s | 1s | 10 | 10 | 9 | 9 | 6 | 6 | 4 | 3 | Shieldhall |

Fare Chart (July 1964)

69. The Riddrie short working terminus was around a large semi-circular area named Tay Crescent, which was neither a specially constructed turning circle, nor a "round the houses" manoeuvre. This terminal point was only a short distance from the Riddrie terminus of Services 101/102/103, but a connection between the two was never made. BUT TB79 waits to return to Bellahouston beside the service numbered bus stop, with Leyland PD2 motorbus L269 on layover to the rear. (R F Mack/S Fozard copyright)

70. The wide Cumbernauld Road stretches up the hill towards Millerston as BUT TB78 passes Riddrie Library, situated at the end of Teith Street. On the opposite side of the road is Tay Crescent, referred to in the previous picture. This vehicle is now preserved at the Sandtoft Trolleybus Museum, North Lincolnshire. (P Mitchell)

71.   BUT TB84 descends Cumbernauld Road as it travels south against the background of inter-war local authority housing stock, and is destined for Bellahouston.  The wide road warranted the use of bracket arms on each side to carry the overhead wiring.  (P Mitchell)

72.   BUT TB64 is just about to turn right into the next section of Cumbernauld Road at its junction with Edinburgh Road.  The large building beyond the Esso sign is the Vogue Bingo Hall, previously The Riddrie cinema.  To the right of TB64 is the site of the ABC Rex cinema, which was demolished post 1973; the two establishments were therefore in sight of each other, an indication why Glasgow was once known as "Cinema City"  The slight hump in the road is a bridge over the ex LMSR goods line north towards Balornock.  (P Mitchell)

73.   With Beatties Vienna Bakery, later known as Dennistoun Bakery, in the background, BUT TB80 travels south west along Cumbernauld Road towards the junction with Duke Street, destined for Bellahouston.  Over the wall is the ex LNER railway line leading north from Duke Street Station towards Springburn.  On the other side of the railway is Paton Street, which led to the bakery and the erstwhile Dennistoun Depot; the latter housed a maximum of eighteen trolleybuses, as well as trams, until its closure in November 1960.  (P Mitchell)

74. The majestic Bellgrove United Presbyterian Church, which was demolished in 1972, forms the backdrop for BUT TB98, as it moves down Bellgrove Street towards Abercromby Street, and onwards to Bellahouston. The cutting to the immediate right of TB98 houses Bellgrove Railway Station. Note that the overhead wiring in the foreground is supported from adjacent traction standards, possibly because of the difficulty of planting the bases for suitable supports near the railway cutting. (P Mitchell)

75. BUT TB73 leaves Bellgrove Street as it crosses Gallowgate, the latter still with tram overhead wiring and track in place, and enters Abercromby Street. Travelling in the opposite direction is BUT TB89, followed by a Morris J delivery van of Millerfield Bakery (famous for their meat pies), with the driver giving a hand signal to turn right. The buildings in the background have made way for modern apartment blocks. (R F Mack/S Fozard copyright)

76.   In spite of the position of the street nameplate attached to the traction standard, BUT TB74 is actually leaving Abercromby Street to enter London Road, and then onwards to Bridgeton Cross and Bellahouston.  Tram track and overhead wiring are still in place, and TB74 is followed by a Rover 75, with an OS (Wigtown 1954/55) registration.  Abercromby Street now joins London Road a little to the left of this view, with the road depicted closed off beyond the line of cars. (P Mitchell)

77.   On a damp day at the same location, but looking in the opposite direction, BUT TB76 begins the turn out of London Road into Abercromby Street, followed by a Leyland motorbus.  All the property looking towards Bridgeton Cross has made way for modern housing.  (P Mitchell)

78. BUT TB78 passes Bridgeton Cross on route to Bellahouston. There was a short working facility at this location, mainly used by trolleybuses at peak times returning to Govan (Lorne School) or Hampden garages. The area under "The Umbrella" bandstand on the right was a regular meeting place, and together with its clock tower, the structure was refurbished a few years ago. "All Quiet on the Western Front" is being shown at the ABC Olympia cinema, rebuilt after a fire as a multi-purpose public building, but retaining the cinema façade as the entrance. The "Snug Bar" on the left is now named "The Seven Ways", reflecting the nature of the road junction here. (R F Mack/S Fozard copyright)

# BRIDGETON CROSS TO PAISLEY ROAD TOLL
## (SERVICE 106)

79. With Bridgeton Cross in the background, BUT TB84 has entered James Street, and is also destined for Bellahouston. The road in the right foreground is Landressy Street, the first leg of the terminal loop, which allowed eastbound trolleybuses to turn short at peak periods to return to their garages, as described in the previous caption. Before the construction of the M8, James Street was the main lorry access to the docks and shipyards; strangely the lorry at the front of the queue loaded with tube, is operating on trade plate 063 XS (Burgh Council of Paisley). (P Mitchell)

➔ 80. BUT TB79 has just left Ballater Street, and is about to cross King's Bridge before entering King's Drive, and onwards to Bridgeton Cross and Millerston in September 1958; the service had opened the previous June. All the buildings to the rear have made way for modern apartments, emphasising the change from former industrial use, illustrated by the metal refining factory on the left. (C Routh)

81. BUT TB62 travels west along the dual carriageway of Ballater Street, with one of the four multi storey apartment blocks adjacent to Waddell Street under construction. The overtaking van is a Ford Thames 10 cwt. (P Mitchell)

82.   With the ex Caledonian/LMSR railway bridge giving access to Glasgow Central Station in the distance, BUT TB59 makes its way along Nelson Street en route to Bellahouston, having just passed Centre Street on the left.   The tall building on the left with a white gable end is the flour mill of William Primrose and Sons.   Note the reverse Guinness advertisement on the right; Nelson Street is now one way in a westerly direction.   (P Mitchell)

83.   At Paisley Road Toll, BUT TB55 leaves Paisley Road, and is about to enter Rutland Place leading into Govan Road, then onwards to Bellahouston.   The overhead wiring leaving the picture on the right led into Admiral Street, which was the second leg of the terminal loop of Service 108 from Mount Florida.   (V Nutton/Travel Lens Photographic)

# PAISLEY ROAD TOLL TO BELLAHOUSTON
## (SERVICE 106)

84.  Having turned the sharp corner in the distance on the eastern side of Princes Dock, BUT TB72 continues along Govan Road adjacent to Mavisbank Quay on its way to Millerston, and followed by a Glasgow Leyland motorbus.  The travelling cranes point skywards, and immediately to their left was the erstwhile passenger/vehicle Harbour Tunnel and Finnieston ferries across the Clyde. This was the site of the 1988 Glasgow Garden Festival.  (P Mitchell)

85.   Having turned the corner referred to in the previous picture, but travelling in the opposite direction to Bellahouston, BUT TB80 has passed under a section insulator, and travels along Govan Road past the end of Craigiehall Street.   The latter still exists, but the junction is now named Craigiehall Place, with a traffic island where TB80 is positioned.   To the left of this picture was the Princes Dock Railway, which led to the basin of the named dock, and other south Clydeside quays. Part of Princes Dock was filled in to create the site for the Garden Festival.   (P Mitchell)

86.   At Govan Cross BUT TB60 makes its way along a damp Govan Road to Bellahouston in May 1964.   The centre set of overhead wiring was for the Fairfield Shipbuilders electric locomotive, which transported goods from the railway goods yard on the right behind the lorry, along the public roadway to the shipyard.   Being rail based, the locomotive used the redundant tram track, drawing power from the central wiring illustrated via two trolleybus style booms, which replaced the earlier bow collector when trams traversed the road.   The bank on the corner of Pearce Street, previously known as Mansfield Street, was once a public house.   (D Smithies)

87.   This picture illustrates the Fairfield Shipyard locomotive using the centre set of overhead wiring, not transporting steel on this occasion, but on an enthusiasts' trip, with the participants seated on the wagons normally used between the railway yard and the shipyard.  The current Health and Safety culture would probably frown on this arrangement.  (Travel Lens Photographic)

88.   BUT TB64 has just turned out of Govan Road into Golspie Street on the last leg of the 9.75 mile (15.7km) journey from Millerston to Bellahouston.  On the opposite side of Govan Road, Howat Street leads down towards the Fairfield Shipbuilders yard, whose cranes dominate the skyline.  (P Mitchell)

89.   BUT TB61 has not quite reached the Bellahouston terminus, but the destination blind has been changed ready for the return journey to Riddrie.  TB61 takes the sharp turn out of Craigton Road into Jura Street, having crossed the bridge over the ex LMSR railway line towards Paisley to the left.  Note that tram track, which is about to be removed.  With the advent of the M8 motorway, Craigton Road is now a cul-de-sac.  (R F Mack/S Fozard copyright)

90. At the Bellahouston terminal stand in Ulva Street, BUT TB82 restarts around the terminal loop to begin the journey to Riddrie. The return leg of the loop towards the city in Jura Street can be seen on the other side of the foliage. (P Mitchell)

## 106 — BELLAHOUSTON to RIDDRIE or MILLERSTON

| Week-days a.m. | a.m. | p.m. | p.m. | a.m. | p.m. | p.m. |
|---|---|---|---|---|---|---|
| 11 25 | | 5 55† | 10 54 | 8 20* | 5 34* | 10 18 |
| 5 22* | 30* | 58* | 11 1 | 24 | 37‡ | 23* |
| 44 | 40 | 6 1† | 3† | 28‡ | 40 | 28 |
| 6 7 | 45* | 4 | 11 | 32* | 43 | 33 |
| 24 | 55 | 7† | 13† | 36 | 46† | 38* |
| 36 | p.m. | 10* | 21 | 40 | 49* | 45 |
| 48 | 12 0* | 13† | 23† | 44* | 52† | 48† |
| 56* | 12 10 | 16 | 28† | 48‡ | 55 | 53 |
| 7 4 | 5 ms | 19† | 33† | 52 | 6 0 | 11 0 |
| 4 ms | 12 15* | 22* | 38† | 56 | 1† | 3† |
| 7 8* | 3 40 | 25† | 43† | 9 0* | 5* | 10 |
| 12 ms* | 45* | 28 | 48† | 15 ms | 7† | 13† |
| 8 16 | 49 | 34* | 55† | 9 5 | 10 | 20 |
| 20* | 55 | 37† | 12 3† | 5 ms | 15 | 23† |
| 24‡ | 58* | 40 | | 10 55 | 20* | 28† |
| 28* | 4 4 | 46* | | 11 0* | 25 | 33† |
| 32‡ | 10* | 49‡ | | 4 | 30 | 39† |
| 36 | 16 | 52 | Sats. | 10 | 35* | 44† |
| 40‡ | 19 | 57* | a.m. | 16 | 40 | 49† |
| 44* | 25 | 7 3 | 5 22* | 22 | 46 | 54† |
| 48‡ | 28 | 7 9* | 44 | 28 | 51* | 59† |
| 52 | 34* | 6 ms | 6 12 | 31* | 56 | 12 4† |
| 56† | 4 37 | Alt. | 24 | 37 | 7 1 | 9† |
| 9 0* | 3 ms | Ridd. | 36 | 43* | 5 ms | 14† |
| 4† | 4 46* | M'ton | 48 | 49 | 7 6* | |
| 8 | 12 ms* | 8 57 | 56* | 55* | 15 ms* | Cont. |
| 16* | 5 19 | 9 3* | 7 4 | 58 | 8 1 | |
| 23 | 22* | 9 | 8* | p.m. | 6* | |
| 30* | 25‡ | 9 19* | 12 | 12 1 | 11 | |
| 9 38 | 15 ms* | 28 | 16 | 12 4 | 16 | |
| 7½ ms | 31‡ | 9 24 | 20* | 3 ms | 22* | |
| Alt. | 34* | 5 ms | 24 | 12 7* | 15 ms* | |
| Ridd. | 10 19* | 28 | 12 ms* | 8 27 | | |
| M'ton | 37† | 24 | 36 | 5 16 | 5 ms | |
| 10 53 | 40 | 29 | 7 40 | 19* | 9 52* | |
| 11 0* | 43† | 34 | 4 ms | 22 | 57 | |
| 10 | 46* | 39† | 7 44* | 25 | 10 3 | |
| 15* | 49‡ | 46 | 12 ms | 28 | 8* | |
| | 52 | 48† | 8 16 | 31‡ | 13 | |

## 106 — BELLAHOUSTON to RIDDRIE or MILLERSTON Cont.

| Sun.s a.m. | a.m. | p.m. | p.m. | p.m. | p.m. | p.m. |
|---|---|---|---|---|---|---|
| 10 40† | 6 ms* | 6 20* | 9 2* | 10 40* | 11 34† | |
| 6 49‡ | 46 | 4 20* | 26* | 8 | 47 | 39† |
| 7 23 | 11 1 | 5 ms* | 32* | 14 | 49† | 42† |
| 40‡ | 16 | 5 40* | 38* | 9 20* | 55 | 47† |
| 8 1 | 31* | 45 | 39† | 15 ms* | 11 2 | 52† |
| 16 | 46* | 50* | 6 44* | 9 25 | 4† | 57† |
| 31 | p.m. | 56* | 6 ms* | 5 ms | 12 | 12 2† |
| 46 | 12 1* | 6 2* | 8 38 | 10 20* | 16† | 10† |
| 9 16 | 16* | 8* | 44 | 25 | 22 | |
| 15 ms | 31* | 9† | 50* | 30* | 24† | |
| 10 31 | 38* | 56 | 56 | 35 | 29† | |

| Unmarked to Riddrie | † To Govan Gar. |
|---|---|
| * To Millerston | ‡ To Bridgeton Cross |

## 106 — MILLERSTON to BELLAHOUSTON

| Week-days a.m. | a.m. | p.m. | a.m. | p.m. | p.m. | p.m. |
|---|---|---|---|---|---|---|
| 15 ms | 11 31† | 11 41 | 15 ms | 12 42 | 6 ms | |
| 6 0 | p.m. | | 53 | 10 35 | 54 | 8 53 |
| 15 | 3 30 | | p.m. | 51 | 1 6 | 9 3 |
| 23 | 44 | Sats. | 12 2 | 11 6 | 1 18 | 5 ms |
| 7 27 | 59 | a.m. | 6 0 | 5 26 | 6 ms | 9 23 |
| 12 ms | 4 14 | 6 0 | 12 ms | 31† | 1 48 | 9 33 |
| 8 27 | 4 41 | 7 27 | 38† | | 1 53 | 15 ms |
| 39† | 12 ms | 12 ms | 6 3 | 50† | 4 23 | 10 48 |
| 51 | 9 5 | 8 51 | 15 ms | Suns. | 5 ms | 11 1 |
| 9 6 | 9 16 | 9 1 | 7 18 | a.m. | 7 5 | 11 |
| 9 14 | 15 ms | 9 15 | 7 34 | 7 5 | 5 53 | 21† |
| 15 ms | 10 46 | 15 ms | 15 ms | | 59 | 31† |
| 10 44 | 11 3 | 11 15 | 9 4 | p.m. | 6 5 | |
| 11 0 | 18 | 9 20 | 30 | 12 24 | 7† | |
| | | | | 6 11 | | |

| Millerston to Riddrie | .. | .. | 5 mins. |
|---|---|---|---|
| Riddrie to Aitken St. | .. | .. | 6 ,, |
| Aitken St. to Bridgeton Cross | .. | .. | 10 ,, |
| Bridgeton Cross to Crown St. | .. | .. | 5 ,, |
| Crown St. to Paisley Rd. Toll | .. | .. | 8 ,, |
| Paisley Rd. Toll to Govan Cross | .. | .. | 8 ,, |
| Govan Cross to Bellahouston | .. | .. | 9 ,, |

† To Govan Gar.  ms Minute Service

Timetable (November 1962)

# MOUNT FLORIDA TO PAISLEY ROAD TOLL
# (SERVICE 108)

91. This service replaced tram Service 12 in November 1958, and was the last UK tram to trolleybus conversion. Ten 34.5ft (10.5m) long single deck trolleybuses, with a setback front axle and single front doorway, were specifically purchased for this suburban service. Ministry of Transport permission was required as the length exceeded the then legal maximum. BUT TBS16 moves along King's Park Road on the last leg of the journey from Paisley Road Toll, and will shortly reach the Mount Florida terminal loop. The exit overhead wiring from the loop can be seen in the background. (P Mitchell)

92.   BUT TBS17 turns out of King's Park Road, and enters the short link into Carmunnock Road, the second leg of the terminal loop; the exit from the loop is in the far distance. The first short link into Carmunnock Road was specially built, and sported a "Trolleybuses only" sign. (Travel Lens Photographic)

93.   On a wet day at the layover stand on the third leg of the 108 terminal loop in Ballogie Road, BUT TBS14 waits ready to return to Paisley Road Toll.  On leaving, TBS14 will turn right into King's Park Road, and onwards to Cathcart Road.  (P Mitchell)

94. A busy mid-afternoon scene, as BUT TBS13 turns out of Cathcart Road into Allison Street to begin its suburban journey across to Paisley Road Toll, with a double deck trolleybus close behind. All the buildings in view still exist. (Author's collection)

### 108 PAISLEY RD TOLL to BALLOGIE RD

| Week-days a.m. | a.m. | p.m. | p.m. | a.m. | a.m. |
|---|---|---|---|---|---|
| 8 15 | 9 19 | 5 21 | 7 10 | 7 45 | 7 32 |
| a.m. | 17 | 24 | 22 | 20 | 7 40 |
| 5 33 | 19 | 9 25 | 26 | 30 | 15 ms |
| 6 2 | 25 | 15 ms | 30 | 40 | 9 10 |
| 13 | 31 | 11 55 | 32 | 7 55 | 10 ms |
| 30 | 36 | p.m. | 38 | 15 ms | 11 30 |
| 43 | 39 | 12 4 | 40 | 9 10 | 45 |
| 54 | 45 | 9 ms | 44 | 10 ms | Suns. |
| 7 7 | 45 | 4 25 | 50 | 11 30 | a.m |
| 17 | 46 | 30 | 55 | 45 | 7 25 |
| 33 | 49 | 38 | 56 | p.m. | 8 11 |
| 39 | 51 | 50 | 6 2 | Sats. | 8 50 |
| 45 | 55 | 58 | 10 | a m | 9 10 |
| 50 | 57 | 5 4 | 20 | 5 33 | 9 25 |
| 51 | 59 | 5 | 25 | 6 6 | 20 ms |
| 54 | 9 5 | 7 | 30 | 32 | p m |
| 57 | 9 | 10 | 35 | 44 | 1 45 |
| 8 3 | 11 | 15 | 40 | 56 | 2 2 |
| 6 | 13 | 16 | 50 | 7 8 | 15 ms |
| 9 | 13 | 18 | 7 0 | 20 | 11 32 |
| 13 | 18 | 20 | 5 | 29 | 45 |
| | | | | 38 | |

*(a.m. 7 45, 53, 8 0, 7½ ms, 9 0, 9 6, 9 ms, 11 39, 47, 55, 12 2, 7½ ms, 3 2, 9, 16, 3 25, 6 52, 7 0, 14, 23)*

### 108 BALLOGIE RD to PAISLEY RD TOLL or LINTHOUSE or SHIELDHALL

| Week-days a.m. | a.m. | p.m. | p.m. | a.m. | p.m. |
|---|---|---|---|---|---|
| 7 30 | 9 5 | 4 32‡ | 6 45 | 7 13 | 9 0 |
| a.m. | 33‡ | 19 | 35† | 50 | 10 ms |
| 5 9 | 39† | 9 30 | 36† | 7 0 | 11 20 |
| 32 | 45† | 15 ms | 42† | 10 | Suns. |
| 53 | 53† | 11 30 | 47 | 20 | a.m. |
| 6 10 | 59† | 39 | 54† | 7 30 | 7 1 |
| 19† | 8 5† | 48 | 58 | 15 ms | 45 |
| 23 | 11§ | 57 | 5 12 | 9 0 | 8 19‡ |
| 29† | 13† | p.m. | 18 | 10 ms | 31 |
| 33 | 16 | 12 6 | 24 | 11 20 | 56 |
| |45‡ | 19† | 9 ms | 30 | | 9 23 |
| 51‡ | 23† | 4 0 | 35 | | 9 45 |
| 57‡ | 26 | 6 | 36 | Sats. | 20 ms |
| 7 |0‡ | 28† | 12† | 42 | a.m. | 9 45 |
| 3‡ | 29 | 14 | 50 | 5 9 | p.m. |
| 9‡ | 33† | 16§ | 6 0 | 32 | 1 25 |
| 11‡ | 35 | 18† | 5 | 6 10 | 35 |
| 13 | 37 | 24† | 10 | 7 12 | 45 |
| 15‡ | 39† | 26‡ | 15 | 34 | 2 7 |
| 18‡ | 45 | 29† | 20 | 46 | 15 ms |
| 23‡ | 51 | 30† | 30 | 58 | 11 22 |
| 27† | 59 | 31§ | 40 | 7 5 | 9 0 |

*(a.m. 7½ ms, 8 43, 50, 59, 9 8, 9 ms, 11 23, 30, 37, 45, 52, 12 0, 5 9, 7½ ms, 3 0, 7 12, 20, 7 30, 58)*

Unmarked to Paisley Rd. Toll   †To Linthouse
§ To Summertown Rd.   ‡ To Shieldhall

| | |
|---|---|
| Ballogie Rd. to Mount Florida .. | 2 mins. |
| Mount Florida to Paisley Rd. Toll | 16 ,, |
| Paisley Rd. Toll to Linthouse .. | 13 ,, |
| Paisley Rd. Toll to Shieldhall .. | 17 ,, |

Timetable (November 1962)

### 108 SHIELDHALL to BALLOGIE ROAD

| Week-days a.m. | a.m. | p.m. | Sats. | Suns. |
|---|---|---|---|---|
| 7 22 | 7 58 | 5 3 | No | a.m. |
| 28 | 8 0 | 9 | Ser-vice | 8 54 |
| 34 | 56 | | | |
| 7 37 | 46 | | | |
| 40 | 49 | | | |
| | 52 | | | |

### 108 LINTHOUSE to BALLOGIE ROAD

| Week-days a.m. | a.m. | a.m. | p.m. | p.m. | Sats. and Suns. |
|---|---|---|---|---|---|
| 6 54 | 8 38 | 9 12 | 4 45 | 5 8 | No Service |
| 7 4 | 12 | 46 | 51 | 9 | |
| 8 0 | 18 | 56 | 57 | 17 | |
| 8 6 | 26 | 9 1 | 5 2 | 27 | |
| | 32 | 6 | 3 | | |

95. On the opposite side of the road, BUT TBS13 is seen again turning out of Allison Street into Cathcart Road on the return to Mount Florida. The Govanhill Parish Church dominates the background, but no longer exists, having been demolished and replaced by a nursery school circa 1975 (also see Picture 50). On the right hand traction standard, the visual indicator displaying the setting of the overhead turnout junction for drivers travelling in the opposite direction can be seen again. (P Mitchell)

96. BUT TBS18 waits at a stop in Allison Street opposite Chapman Street, outwards to Paisley Road Toll. In the distance is Victoria Cross, where Services 5/107 crossed at 90 degrees along Victoria Road. A Ford Thames Trader is about to overtake, and the building on the right overlooking Craigie Street School playground, still includes the large advertisement frame on the gable end. (R F Mack/ S Fozard copyright)

97. Destined for Mount Florida, BUT TBS20 moves along Allison Street past the end of Craigie Street on the right. The fire station on the left was known as Queen's Park Fire Station, which after closure in 1987, was combined with the South Fire Station to form Polmadie Fire Station; the building still exists. (S Lockwood collection)

98. Further along Allison Street, BUT TBS19 passes the end of Niddrie Road, destined for Mount Florida. Pollokshaws Road crosses in the background at Nithsdale Street. (Author's collection)

99.  A double decker on Service 108 destined for Paisley Road Toll.  Having left Nithsdale Street, BUT TB37 has entered Nithsdale Road and crosses the railway bridge at the former St Strathbumgo Station, next to Darnley Road.  The railway line under the bridge provided access to Glasgow Central Station, and earlier, the erstwhile St Enoch's Station.  (S Lockwood collection)

100.  BUT TBS14 has climbed Shields Road from Paisley Road Toll, and is about to cross Albert Drive on the return to Mount Florida.  It has just passed under a section insulator, again identified by the white bands on the traction standards, with power to the overhead being fed from the Car Works substation.  Tram track crosses leading towards Pollokshields and Bellahouston Park on the left.  The turreted building on the left is now obscured by heavy foliage.
(R F Mack/S Fozard copyright)

101. Having left the terminal loop at Paisley Road Toll, BUT TBS12 has travelled along Milnpark Street, Seaward Street and Scotland Street to join Shields Road, roughly where the current M8 passes over the location. There is a sharp incline up Shields Road to just before Albert Drive, which TBS12 is tackling on the return to Hampden Garage. (P Mitchell)

102. BUT TBS1 is seen here at Paisley Road Toll on an enthusiasts' special, having just turned out of Seaward Street into Paisley Road. The crossover of overhead wiring, which applied from May 1959, allowed vehicles on Service 108 to cross to the outer wiring leading into Rutland Place and Govan Road, to provide workmen's specials to Linthouse and Shieldhall. The second leg of the crossover allowed vehicles approaching from Paisley Road to cross to the inner wiring, and thus provide a short working around the 108 Paisley Road Toll terminal loop; the return wiring into Paisley Road can be seen in the background. A Scammell Scarab with trailer overtakes double deck BUT TB72, with the erstwhile Woolworth store on the right. (R F Mack/NTA)

**Trolleybus Service No. 108**

## SHIELDHALL or LINTHOUSE or PAISLEY ROAD TOLL and MOUNT FLORIDA

**No Weekly Tickets**

| Stage No. | | | | | | | | | | | | |
|---|---|---|---|---|---|---|---|---|---|---|---|---|
| 37 | Shieldhall (Renfrew Road at Shieldhall Road) | | | | | | | | | | | |
| 36 | 3 | Bogmoor Road | | | | | | | | | | |
| 35 | 4 | 3 | Govan Road at Moss Road (Linthouse Ter.) | | | | | | | | | |
| 34 | 6 | 4 | 3 | Govan Cross | | | | | | | | |
| 33 | 6 | 6 | 4 | 3 | Summertown Road | | | | | | | |
| 32 | 9 | 6 | 6 | 4 | 3 | Lorne School | | | | | | |
| 31 | 9 | 9 | 6 | 6 | 4 | 3 | Paisley Road Toll | | | | | |
| 30 | 10 | 9 | 9 | 6 | 6 | 4 | 3 | Albert Drive | | | | |
| 29 | 10 | 10 | 9 | 9 | 6 | 6 | 4 | 3 | Pollokshaws Road | | | |
| 28 | 1s | 10 | 10 | 9 | 9 | 6 | 6 | 4 | 3 | Dixon Avenue | | |
| 27 | 1s | 1s | 10 | 10 | 9 | 9 | 6 | 6 | 4 | 3 | Mount Florida | |
| 26 | 1s | 1s | 1s | 10 | 10 | 9 | 9 | 6 | 6 | 4 | 3 | Ballogie Road |
| 25 | 1s | 1s | 1s | 1s | 10 | 10 | 9 | 9 | 6 | 6 | 4 | 3 | Hampden Gar. |

Fare Chart (July 1964)

103. This view at the same location depicts BUT TBS12 traversing the terminal loop in May 1964, having just left Seaward Street, and is about to enter Admiral Street to reach the terminal stand. The destination blind has already been changed ready for the return to Mount Florida. The crossover connections have been removed, to be replaced by a connection from Seaward Street to the westbound wiring into Rutland Place and Govan Road. The connection can just be seen in the distance, which allowed vehicles on Service 108 to continue onwards to Linthouse and Shieldhall for workmen's specials. (D Smithies)

104. Having reached Admiral Street, BUT TBS21 waits at the terminal stand ready for the return to Mount Florida. On leaving, it will turn into the last leg of the terminal loop, namely Milnpark Street, before regaining Seaward Street, and then onwards to Shields Road. To the rear, a Post Office van waits outside the local Post Office, which no longer exists, although the post box and a modern telephone box remain at the time of writing. (V Nutton/Travel Lens Photographic)

105. At the same location, a lady steps down from the narrow doorway of BUT TBS20 in May 1964. This single doorway was the main weakness of this batch of trolleybuses, which led to excessive loading and unloading times. TBS20 has used the nearside overhead wiring out of Paisley Road, with the offside wiring leading in from Govan Road and Rutland Place on the left. To the rear, on the other side of the road, was the entrance to the ex LMSR Goods Yard, next to General Terminus Quay, now given over to modern housing. (D Smithies)

# OUTWARDS TO LINTHOUSE AND SHIELDHALL
## (SERVICES 106/108)

*Services 106 and 108 were extended to Linthouse and Shieldhall to cater for workmen's specials at shift change times.*

106. In Govan Road, Linthouse, Sunbeam TG14 is pictured on a workmen's extension of Service 106 to Shieldhall. Immediately in front of the Sunbeam is the overhead turnout junction for the Linthouse terminal loop, leading into Moss Road. Most of the advertisements adorning the newsagents shop are for tobacco products, although Lucozade could be purchased. Some of the buildings in the distance were demolished to make way for the approach roads to the new Clyde Tunnel, opened in 1963. (P Mitchell)

107.   BUT TBS12 has turned out of Govan Road into Moss Road to start around the Linthouse terminal loop, on an extension of Service 108.   On the left is the site of the current Queen Elizabeth University Hospital complex, the Southern General Hospital as it was in this view.   The shipbuilding premises of Alexander Stephen and Sons, where Billy Connolly served his apprenticeship, dominate the background, but now a new Linthouse Road cuts across the vacated site, leading to the Thales Optronics factory.   (P Mitchell)

← 108. On the second leg of the Linthouse terminal loop, BUT TBS11 enters Peninver Drive on an extension of Service 108, followed by BUT TB37 turning out of Moss Road on an extension of Service 106. The buildings on the right still exist, although the established trees in the background have disappeared. (P Mitchell)

109. In this view BUT TB38 has reached the Shieldhall terminus, which was around the traffic island at the junction of Renfrew and Shieldhall Roads. TB38 is returning to Hampden Garage having completed the workmen's special of extended Service 108, as a Ford Consul follows close behind. (P Mitchell)

# ROLLING STOCK

## Liveries

| Double Deck | 1 | 2 | 3 | 4 |
|---|---|---|---|---|
| Roof | Cream Later Green | Green | Green | Green |
| Upper Window Surround | Cream | Green | Green | Green |
| Band | Orange | - | - | - |
| Between Decks | Cream | Cream | Cream | Green |
| Band | Orange | - | - | Cream |
| Lower Window Surround | Cream | Green | Green | Yellow |
| Band | Cream | Cream | - | - |
| Lower Panels | Green | Orange | Orange | Yellow |

| Single Deck | A | B | C | D |
|---|---|---|---|---|
| Roof | Cream | Green | Green | Green |
| Band | Green | - | - | - |
| Window Surround | Cream | Green | Green | Cream |
| Band | Cream | Cream | Cream | Green |
| Lower Panels | Orange | Orange | Yellow | Orange |

*The above indicates the basic livery changes, but there were minor variations and experimental exceptions.*

110.    **1949   TB1 – 34   BUT 9641T   FYS 701 – 734**
**Liveries 1 > 2 > 3 > 4**

This batch was the first delivery of trolleybuses for the opening of the system, with chassis produced by AEC under the BUT branding established following the merger of Leyland and AEC trolleybus interests. TB1 – 32 were fitted with English Electric motors, whilst those for TB33/34 were supplied by Crompton Parkinson. The bodies were produced by MCCW, and seated 70. In order to expedite early delivery, the bodies were produced at the end of a production run of London Transport Q1 trolleybuses, and were to the same design. A chassis was exhibited at the 1948 Commercial Motor Show, and a completed TB32 at the British Industries Fair in 1949. TB22 is seen in the Hampden garage yard. There were two withdrawals by 1961, with the remainder disappearing between 1962 and 1966; not all vehicles were in the final livery. (S Lockwood collection)

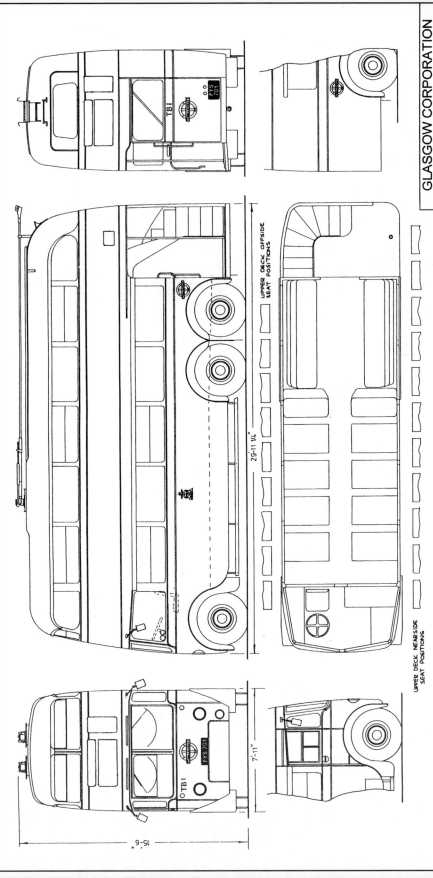

## GLASGOW CORPORATION
## D/DECK 3 AXLE TROLLEYBUS

Body: Met-Cam 1949.
Chassis: B.U.T. 9641T
Fleet No. TB1 –TB34

Scale:
4mm = 1 Foot

## DRAWING No. TB88

UPPER DECK OFFSIDE
SEAT POSITIONS

29-11 1/4"

UPPER DECK NEARSIDE
SEAT POSITIONS

7-11"

15'-6"

SCALE
FEET    0   1   2   3   4   5   6   7   8   9   10  11  12

Note: London Transport style trolleybus roundels subsequently removed
and front fleet number moved to central position.

AVAILABLE FROM: TERRY RUSSELL, 23, THORNDEN, COWFOLD, HORSHAM, WEST SUSSEX,
RH13 8AG FOR THE FULL LIST OF OVER 1000 DRAWINGS AND MODEL TRAM PARTS VISIT MY
WEB SITE www.terryrusselltrams.co.uk OR SEND 6 FIRST CLASS STAMPS FOR A PAPER COPY.

**111.   1949/50   TD1 – 30   Daimler CTM6   FYS 735 – 764**
**Liveries 1 > 2 > 3 > 4**

This was the follow on delivery, also with 70 seat bodies by MCCW to an identical London Transport Q1 design; only the front wings were slightly different to the vehicle in the previous picture. This batch was fitted with Metrovick motors, and TD13 was fitted with a single boom for a short period; in addition TD22 was fitted with boom retrievers for a period in 1953/54.  TD9 crosses Victoria Bridge over the River Clyde travelling north on a short working of Service 105 to Maitland Street. The batch was withdrawn between 1958 and 1964; not all vehicles were in the final livery.
(S Lockwood collection)

**112.   1951   TBS1 (originally TB35)   BUT RETB1   FYS 765**
**Liveries A > B > C**

This experimental single deck vehicle was based on a shortened version of Leyland's 33ft (9.6m) long export chassis, and fitted with a Metrovick motor. The body was by Weymann, and comprised a rear entrance, which led into a circulating area in front of a seated conductor. 26 seats were provided, with space for 40 standing passengers, later reduced to 30; the exit door was in front of the set back front axle. The concept was not entirely successful, and the conductor's desk/rear entrance were removed to provide a total of 36 seats. In its original form, it was demonstrated on the trolleybus system of South Lancashire Traction based in Atherton, plus it operated in Edinburgh using a single boom to the tram positive overhead wiring, with a skate running in the tram track to provide a negative return. The vehicle was exhibited at the 1950 Commercial Motor Show, withdrawn in 1964, and is seen here when on display in Edinburgh. (Omnibus Society copyright)

113. **1953 TBS2 – 11 BUT RETB1 FYS 766 – 775**
**Liveries B > C**

This was the bulk delivery following operation of the vehicle in the previous picture, and they were fitted with dual entrance/exit bodes by East Lancashire Coachbuilders, seating 27, and originally accommodating 40 "standees", subsequently reduced to 30. However the exit was wider, and positioned to the rear of the front axle. The batch was subsequently rebuilt by the removal of the conductor's desk and rear entrance to accommodate 36 seated passengers. English Electric motors were fitted, and a chassis was exhibited at the 1952 Commercial Motor Show. TBS2 was demonstrated on the Nottingham and Walsall systems before delivery to Glasgow, and the batch was withdrawn in 1964. TBS2 is seen here whilst in Walsall; the wording on the building gable end reads "Walsall Corporation Motors". (R Marshall/Omnibus Society copyright)

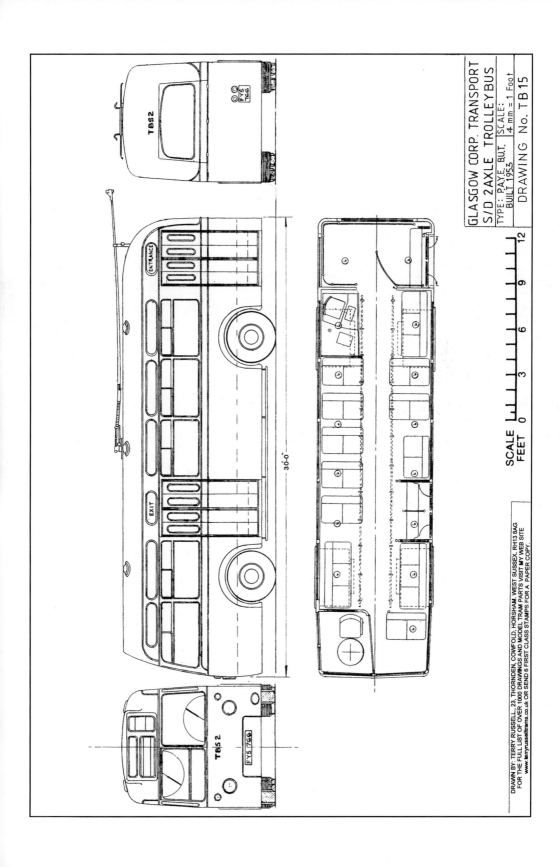

GLASGOW CORP. TRANSPORT
S/D 2 AXLE TROLLEY BUS

TYPE: P.A.Y.E. B.U.T. | SCALE:
BUILT 1953. | 4 mm = 1 Foot

DRAWING No. T B 15

SCALE
FEET  0   3   6   9   12

TB52

FYS 766

30'-0"

ENTRANCE

EXIT

DRAWN BY: TERRY RUSSELL, 23, THORNDEN, COWFOLD, HORSHAM, WEST SUSSEX, RH13 8AG
FOR THE FULL LIST OF OVER 1000 DRAWINGS AND MODEL TRAM PARTS VISIT MY WEB SITE
www.terryrusselltrams.co.uk OR SEND 6 FIRST CLASS STAMPS FOR A PAPER COPY.

**114.  1953  TG1 – 5  SUNBEAM F4A**
    **FYS766 – 780    Liveries 2 > 4**

→  **115.  1953  TG6 – 20  SUNBEAM F4A**
      **FYS 781 – 795    Liveries 3 > 4**

The next five vehicles arrived with 62 seat bodies by Scottish bodybuilder Walter Alexander, who only ever built six trolleybus bodies, the additional one being for South Yorkshire PTE's experimental Dennis trolleybus.  TG1 was exhibited at the 1952 Commercial Motor Show fitted with a single boom, but this was transferred to TD13 before the former entered service.  Although of Sunbeam manufacture, the G designation in the fleet number referred to Guy Motors, who were the parent company, as the letter S had already been used for the single deck fleet.  English Electric motors were fitted, and withdrawal came in 1965; TG5 is seen at the Riddrie terminus of Service 101, the only vehicle from this batch not to receive the final livery. (V Nutton/Travel Lens Photographic)

The remainder of this chassis order were bodied by Weymann, again with 62 seats, and incorporating a nearside cab door.  English Electric motors were specified, and TG6 was fitted with boom retrievers from TD22 for a four year period commencing in 1954.  Withdrawals were during 1965/66, and two vehicles were never painted in the final livery.  TG9 travels south along Castle Street on Service 102 to Polmadie. (R F Mack/NTA)

↓  116.  **1957/58**  **TB35 – 124**  **BUT 9613T**  **FYS 796 – 875 (TB35 – 114)**
**FYS 977 – 986 (TB115 – 124)**

**Motors**  **General Electric**  **TB35 – 64   70 Seats**
**Metrovick**  **TB65 – 124   71 Seats**
**Liveries 3 > 4**

This large bulk order was bodied by Crossley. A chassis was exhibited at the 1956 Commercial Motor Show, and TB107 at the same event in 1958. TB35 – 114 had seating increased to 71 in 1960/61, and TB121 was fitted with boom retrievers from 1958 to 1961.  The first withdrawals were in 1965, and the remainder in 1966/67. TB78 can be seen at the Sandtoft Trolleybus Museum, North Lincolnshire.  TB116 is seen at Hampden Garage in June 1967.  Not all vehicles were in the final livery.  (D Smithies)

**117.  1958   TBS12 – 21   BUT RETB1   FYS 987 – 996**
**Livery D**

These 34.5ft (10.5m) long export chassis required Ministry of Transport permission to operate on the suburban Service 108 from Mount Florida to Paisley Road Toll.  The bodies were by Burlingham, seating 50, but were built with a single narrow front doorway, which had an adverse effect on boarding and alighting time.  Metrovick motors were fitted, and TBS13 (wrongly numbered TBS3) was exhibited at the 1958 Commercial Motor Show; boom retrievers were fitted to TBS14 for about a two year period.  The majority were withdrawn in 1966/67, with two earlier casualties in 1961 and 1964.  TBS15 passes Paisley Road Toll on a workmen's extension of Service 108 to Linthouse.  TBS13 is the sole survivor, and is currently held in Glasgow Museum's Nitshill store,  TBS21 was originally saved, but is now scrapped.  (S Lockwood collection)

# TOWER WAGONS

118.   At its peak, the Overhead Line Department operated ten maroon painted tower wagons comprising six Albions from 1939/40 (DGB 98/184/222/337/561/709), and four Bedfords delivered in 1949/50 (FGG 595/596 and GYS 351/HGA 502).  These vehicles covered both tram and trolleybus overhead wiring infrastructure.  Bedford FGG 595 from the post war delivery is illustrated; the four later vehicles were fitted with radios.  (Author's collection)

# GARAGES

*Trolleybuses operated out of four garages, with three in use between June 1958 and November 1960.*

**Larkfield** was a purpose built bus garage, which opened in 1929, with an overhaul works erected next door opening in 1941. The garage was used for a short period by trolleybuses when the system opened in 1949, pending the completion of the specially commissioned trolleybus garage at Hampden. Approximately 58 trolleybuses could be accommodated, and occupancy was from April 1949 to December 1950, when vehicles were then transferred to Hampden. In later years, the facility was used by First Bus.

**Hampden** was opened in December 1950, and was next to the Hampden Park Stadium. It could accommodate 135 trolleybuses and, to minimise the amount of overhead wiring, the parking area was built on a slope, thus enabling vehicles to manoeuvre by a combination of "freewheeling", and battery power. It closed in May 1967, and the site is now a Park and Ride facility.

**Dennistoun** opened in 1896 as a depot for horse trams, and was later extended for electric trams. A maximum of 18 trolleybuses could be accommodated from June 1958, together with the resident trams; when tram Service 23 ceased, the facility was closed in November 1960. The trolleybuses were re-allocated to Govan and Hampden garages, and the site subsequently sold to an adjacent bakery.

**Govan** opened in 1915 for electric trams. From June 1958, the garage could accommodate a maximum of 55 trolleybuses, from which they operated until October 1966. Motorbuses were also housed from 1962, and continued to operate out of the facility until 1969, when the garage closed.

119. This view of Hampden Garage parking area has BUTs TB116 and TB39 in the foreground, plus nine single deckers on the left. The traction standards have white areas to assist the drivers when parking, and in the background is the embankment of Hampden Park Stadium. (D Smithies)

# THE END

The last day of trolleybus operation was 27th May 1967 and, during the previous week, BUTs TB78 and TB123 were decorated, including large external posters announcing the "Last Trolleybus Week". On this last day, these two vehicles were used by the STMS for tours of the system. In addition, one of the long single deckers, namely TBS21, was used by the NTA; this latter vehicle strayed from its normal Service 108 suburban territory. The final journey from Queen's Cross had TB105, the last vehicle in public service, leading TB123, TBS21 and tower wagon HGA 502 to Hampden Garage. On the following day, TB123 left the garage under battery power, but with booms raised; after a halt for photographers, overhead power was unexpectedly restored with TB123 then travelling to Gorbals Cross to await a towing vehicle.

120. Here we see a rear view of the two decorated trolleybuses in Hampden Garage, namely TB78 in the foreground and TB123 beyond. Pennants have been attached to the booms, together with the "Last Trolleybus Week" posters, which were designed by Brian Deans in conjunction with Publicity Officer Tom McLeod, announcing the impending closure of the system. The round sign in the lower rear window of TB123 was the logo of the STMS, whose members used the vehicle for their last trolleybus journey. (Travel Lens Photographic)

# Middleton Press

**Easebourne Lane, Midhurst, West Sussex**
**GU29 9AZ  Tel:01730 813169**
**email:info@middletonpress.co.uk**

ISBN PREFIXES - A-978 0 906520  B- 978 1 873793  C- 978 1 901706  D-978 1 904474  E - 978 1 906008  F - 978 1 908174

**\* BROCHURE AVAILABLE SHOWING RAILWAY ALBUMS AND NEW TITLES \***
**ORDER ONLINE - *PLEASE VISIT OUR WEBSITE* - www.middletonpress.co.uk**

## TRAMWAY CLASSICS  *Editor Robert J Harley*

| | |
|---|---|
| Aldgate & Stepney Tramways to Hackney and West India Docks | B 70 1 |
| Barnet & Finchley Tramways to Golders Green and Highgate | B 93 0 |
| Bath Tramways  Peter Davey and Paul Welland | B 86 2 |
| Blackpool Tramways 1933-66 75 years of Streamliners  Stephen Lockwood | E 34 5 |
| Bournemouth & Poole Tramways  Roy C Anderson | B 47 3 |
| Brightons Tramways The Corporation's routes plus lines to Shoreham and to Rottingdean | B 02 2 |
| Bristol's Tramways A massive system radiating to ten destinations  Peter Davey | B 57 2 |
| Burton & Ashby Tramways An often rural light railway  Peter M White | C 51 2 |
| Camberwell & West Norwood Trys including Herne Hill and Peckham Rye | B 22 0 |
| Chester Tramways Barry M Marsden | E 04 8 |
| Chesterfield Tramways a typical provincial system  Barry Marsden | D 37 1 |
| Clapham & Streatham Tramways including Tooting and Earlsfield  J.Gent & J.Meredith | B 97 8 |
| Croydons Tramways J.Gent & J.Meredith  including Crystal Palace, Mitcham and Sutton | B 42 8 |
| Derby Tramways a comprehensive city system  Colin Barker | D 17 3 |
| Dover's Tramways to River and Maxton | B 24 4 |
| East Ham & West Ham Trys from Stratford and Ilford down to the docks | B 52 7 |
| Edgware & Willesden Tramways including Sudbury, Paddington & Acton | C 18 5 |
| Eltham & Woolwich Tramways | B 74 9 |
| Embankment & Waterloo Trys including the fondly remembered Kingsway Subway | B 41 1 |
| Enfield and Wood Green Tramways  Dave Jones | C 03 1 |
| Exeter & Taunton Tramways Two charming small systems  J B Perkin | B 32 9 |
| Fulwell - Home for Trams, Trolleys and Buses  Professor Bryan Woodriff | D 11 1 |
| Gosport & Horndean Tramways Martin Petch | B 92 3 |
| Great Yarmouth Tramways A seaside pleasure trip  Dave Mackley | D 13 5 |
| Hammersmith & Hounslow Trys branches to Hanwell, Acton & Shepherds Bush | C 33 8 |
| Hampstead & Highgate Trys from Tottenham Court Road and King's Cross  Dave Jones | B 53 4 |
| Hastings Tramways  A sea front and rural ride | B 18 3 |
| Holborn & Finsbury Trys Angel-Balls Pond Road - Moorgate - Bloomsbury | B 79 4 |
| Huddersfield Tramways the original municipal system  Stephen Lockwood | D 95 1 |
| Hull Tramways Level crossings and bridges abound  Paul Morfitt & Malcolm Wells | D 60 9 |
| Ilford & Barking Tramways to Barkingside, Chadwell Heath and Beckton | B 61 9 |
| Ilkeston & Glossop Tramways  Barry M Marsden | D 40 1 |
| Ipswich Tramways  Colin Barker | E 55 0 |
| Keighley Tramways & Trolleybuses  Barry M Marsden | D 83 8 |
| Kingston & Wimbledon Trys incl Hampton Court, Tooting & four routes from Kingston | B 56 5 |
| Liverpool Tramways - 1  Eastern Routes | C 04 8 |
| Liverpool Tramways - 2 Southern Routes | C 23 9 |
| Liverpool Tramways - 3 Northern Routes  A triliogy by Brian Martin | C 46 8 |
| Llandudno & Colwyn Bay Tramways  Stephen Lockwood | E 17 8 |
| Lowestoft Tramways a seaside system  David Mackley | E 74 1 |
| Maidstone & Chatham Trys from Barming to Loose and from Strood to Rainham | B 40 4 |
| Margate & Ramsgate Tramways including Broadstairs | C 52 9 |
| North Kent Tramways including Bexley, Erith, Dartford, Gravesend and Sheerness | B 44 2 |
| Norwich Tramways A popular system comprising ten main routes  David Mackley | C 40 6 |
| Nottinghamshire & Derbyshire Try including the Matlock Cable Tramway  Barry M Marsden | D 53 1 |
| Plymouth and Torquay Trys including Babbacombe Cliff Lift  Roy Anderson | E 97 0 |
| Portsmouth Tramways including Southsea  Martin Petch | B 72 5 |
| Reading  Tramways Three routes - a comprehensive coverage  Edgar Jordon | B 87 9 |

| | |
|---|---|
| Scarborough Tramway including the Scarborough Cliff Lifts  Barry M Marsden | E |
| Seaton & Eastbourne Tramways  Attractive miniature lines | B |
| Shepherds Bush & Uxbridge Tramways including Ealing  John C Gillham | C |
| Southend-on-Sea Tramways including the Pier Electric Railway | B |
| South London Tramways 1903-33 Wandsworth - Dartford | D |
| South London Tramways 1933-52  The Thames to Croydon | D |
| Southampton Tramways Martin Petch | B |
| Southwark & Deptford Tramways including the Old Kent Road | B |
| Stamford Hill Tramways including Stoke Newington and Liverpool Street | B |
| Thanets Tramways | B |
| Triumphant Tramways of England  Stephen Lockwood  **FULL COLOUR** | C |
| Twickenham & Kingston Trys extending to Richmond Bridge and Wimbledon | C |
| Victoria & Lambeth Tramways to Nine Elms, Brixton and Kennington | B |
| Waltham Cross & Edmonton Trys to Finsbury Park, Wood Green and Enfield | B |
| Walthamstow & Leyton Trys including Clapton, Chingford Hill and Woodford | C |
| Wandsworth & Battersea Trys from Hammersmith, Putney and Chelsea | B |
| York Tramways & Trolleybuses  Barry M Marsden | D |

## TROLLEYBUSES  *(all limp covers)*

| | |
|---|---|
| Birmingham Trolleybuses ... David Harvey | E |
| Bournemouth Trolleybuses ... Malcolm N Pearce | C |
| Bradford Trolleybuses ... Stephen Lockwood | D |
| Brighton Trolleybuses ... Andrew Henbest | D |
| Cardiff Trolleybuses ... Stephen Lockwood | D |
| Chesterfield Trolleybuses ... Barry M Marsden | D |
| Croydon Trolleybuses ... Terry Russell | C |
| Darlington Trolleybuses ... Stephen Lockwood | E |
| Derby Trolleybuses ... Colin Barker | C |
| Doncaster Trolleybuses ... Colin Barker | E |
| Glasgow Trolleybuses ... Colin Barker | F |
| Grimsby & Cleethorpes Trolleybuses ... Colin Barker | D |
| Hastings Trolleybuses ... Lyndon W Rowe | D |
| Huddersfield Trolleybuses ... Stephen Lockwood | C |
| Hull Trolleybuses ... Paul Morfitt and Malcolm Wells | D |
| Ipswich Trolleybuses ... Colin Barker | D |
| Maidstone Trolleybuses ... Robert J Harley | D |
| Manchester & Ashton Trolleybuses ... Stephen Lockwood | D |
| Mexborough & Swinton Trolleybuses ... Colin Barker | D |
| Newcastle Trolleybuses ... Stephen Lockwood | D |
| Nottingham Trolleybuses ... Colin Barker | F |
| Nottinghamshire & Derbyshire Trolleybuses ... Barry M Marsden | D |
| Portsmouth Trolleybuses ... Barry Cox | C |
| Reading Trolleybuses ... David Hall | C |
| Rotherham Trolleybuses ... Colin Barker | |
| Southend Trolleybuses ... Colin Barker | |
| South Lancashire Trolleybuses ... Stephen Lockwood | |
| South Shields Trolleybuses ... Stephen Lockwood | |
| St. Helens Trolleybuses ... Stephen Lockwood | |
| Tees-side Trolleybuses ... Stephen Lockwood | |
| Walsall Trolleybuses ... Stephen Lockwood | |
| Wolverhampton Trolleybuses 1961-67 ... Graham Sidwell | |
| Woolwich and Dartford Trolleybuses ... Robert J Harley | |